# TERRIFIC PAPER TOYS

## E. Richard Churchill

*Illustrated by James Michaels*

 Sterling Publishing Co., Inc.   New York

This book is dedicated to wonderful friends, Bob and Marilyn Collins, and Jack and Beryl Collins, who fill our lives with cheer and love. Who could ask for finer friends?

**Edited by Keith L. Schiffman**

**Library of Congress Cataloging-in-Publication Data**

Churchill, E. Richard (Elmer Richard)
    Terrific paper toys / by E. Richard Churchill ; illustrated by James Michaels.
        p.   cm.
    Summary: Shows how to make a variety of paper toys, including party hats, puppets, flowers, and decorative chains.
    ISBN 0-8069-7496-6
    1. Paper toys—Juvenile literature.  [1. Paper toys.
2. Handicraft.]  I. Michaels, James, ill.   II. Title
TT870.C546   1991
745.592—dc20                                                        90-24115
                                                                                    CIP
                                                                                    AC

10   9   8   7   6   5   4   3   2   1

© 1991 by E. Richard Churchill
Published by Sterling Publishing Company, Inc.
387 Park Avenue South, New York, N.Y. 10016
Distributed in Canada by Sterling Publishing
c/o Canadian Manda Group, P.O. Box 920, Station U
Toronto, Ontario, Canada M8Z 5P9
Distributed in Great Britain and Europe by Cassell PLC
Villiers House, 41/47 Strand, London WC2N 5JE, England
Distributed in Australia by Capricorn Ltd.
P.O. Box 665, Lane Cove, NSW 2066

*Manufactured in the United States of America*
*All rights reserved*

Sterling ISBN 0-8069-7496-6   Trade

# Contents

# Metric Equivalents

INCHES TO MILLIMETRES AND CENTIMETRES

*MM—millimetres    CM—centimetres*

| Inches | MM | CM | Inches | CM | Inches | CM |
|--------|-----|------|--------|------|--------|-------|
| ⅛ | 3 | 0.3 | 9 | 22.9 | 30 | 76.2 |
| ¼ | 6 | 0.6 | 10 | 25.4 | 31 | 78.7 |
| ⅜ | 10 | 1.0 | 11 | 27.9 | 32 | 81.3 |
| ½ | 13 | 1.3 | 12 | 30.5 | 33 | 83.8 |
| ⅝ | 16 | 1.6 | 13 | 33.0 | 34 | 86.4 |
| ¾ | 19 | 1.9 | 14 | 35.6 | 35 | 88.9 |
| ⅞ | 22 | 2.2 | 15 | 38.1 | 36 | 91.4 |
| 1 | 25 | 2.5 | 16 | 40.6 | 37 | 94.0 |
| 1¼ | 32 | 3.2 | 17 | 43.2 | 38 | 96.5 |
| 1½ | 38 | 3.8 | 18 | 45.7 | 39 | 99.1 |
| 1¾ | 44 | 4.4 | 19 | 48.3 | 40 | 101.6 |
| 2 | 51 | 5.1 | 20 | 50.8 | 41 | 104.1 |
| 2½ | 64 | 6.4 | 21 | 53.3 | 42 | 106.7 |
| 2 | 76 | 7.6 | 22 | 55.9 | 43 | 109.2 |
| 3½ | 89 | 8.9 | 23 | 58.4 | 44 | 111.8 |
| 4 | 102 | 10.2 | 24 | 61.0 | 45 | 114.3 |
| 4½ | 114 | 11.4 | 25 | 63.5 | 46 | 116.8 |
| 5 | 127 | 12.7 | 26 | 66.0 | 47 | 119.4 |
| 6 | 152 | 15.2 | 27 | 68.6 | 48 | 121.9 |
| 7 | 178 | 17.8 | 28 | 71.1 | 49 | 124.5 |
| 8 | 203 | 20.3 | 29 | 73.7 | 50 | 127.0 |

# GETTING READY TO MAKE TERRIFIC PAPER TOYS

The terrific paper toys described in this book are not difficult to make. Just follow the instructions one step at a time and you'll end up with paper toys exactly like the ones shown.

You won't have to go out and buy lots of expensive or hard-to-find items in order to make these toys. They are made from materials you have around the house. Notebook paper, typing paper, and newspaper are often used. Sometimes you may want to use gift-wrapping paper to brighten up the finished toy.

Some of the terrific paper toys need to be made of material stiffer than paper. For these cereal box cardboard is perfect. File cards and file folders sometimes come in handy.

Of course, you'll need a pair of scissors to cut the paper and cereal boxes. Cellophane tape or masking tape, or glue are all needed at times to hold things together. For a few toys, paper fasteners are great, but if you don't have them handy, the directions will explain how to make paper clips work just as well. If you have a stapler, there may be times you'd use it rather than tape or glue.

Color crayons or paints come in handy for some toys. Naturally, you'll need a pencil and a ruler from time to time. When any other tools or materials are needed, the directions will tell you. These supplies won't be difficult to find around the house.

It's a great idea to keep your equipment and supplies in one place (such as your desk) so you don't have to look for the scissors each time you want to make another terrific paper toy. Begin to save cereal boxes right now, so you'll have a supply when you need them. Don't let them clutter up your room, or where ever else you work on these toys.

Why not start your toymaking at the beginning of the book? Later, if you wish, feel free to skip around and make the toys in any order you choose.

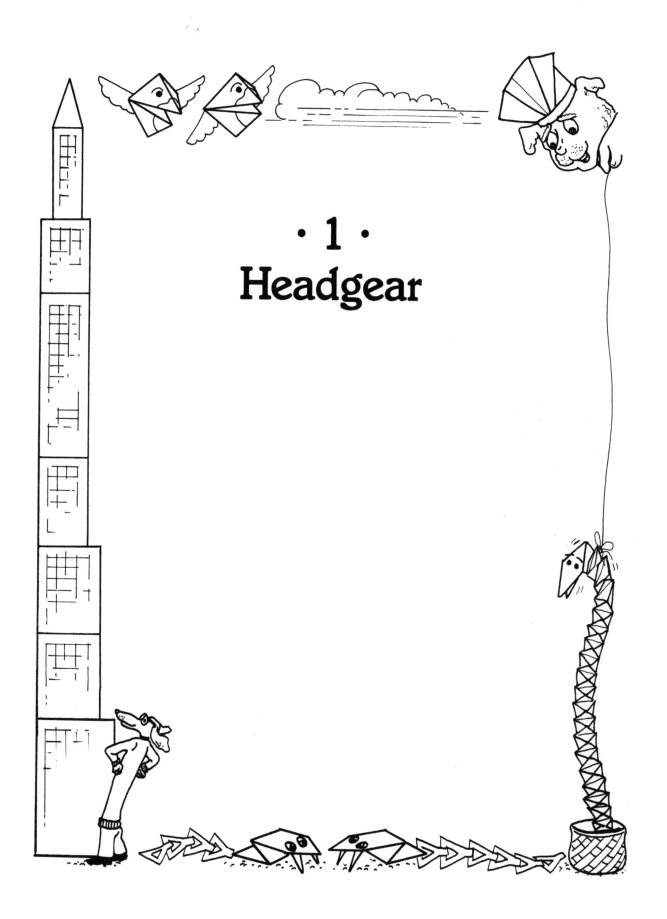

# · 1 ·
# Headgear

# HEADGEAR

We wear hats and caps for many reasons. They keep the sun off our heads and out of our eyes or hold our hair in place when the wind is blowing. Helmets protect football players. Fire fighters wear special headgear for safety reasons. Kings and queens wear crowns as a sign of their high position—at least they used to.

The headgear in this chapter is for fun. Some of the hats are great at parties. Others are wonderful because they are attention-getting. You can make these hats and caps small enough for dolls to wear or large enough for you. They are great when you want to make a toy for a younger child.

## Viking Special

You've seen pictures of Viking helmets with horns sticking up from both sides. The *Viking Special* gives you a terrific piece of headgear with two points extending out from either side. If you don't want to be a Viking, you can still wear this great paper helmet with the points towards the front and back—no one will ever mistake you for a Viking.

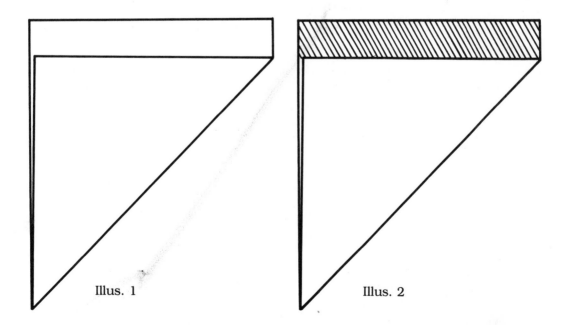

Illus. 1                    Illus. 2

If this hat is going to be large enough for you to wear, you'll need a double page of newspaper from one of the large-sized newspapers, not from a smaller tabloid size.

Before you make a full-sized *Viking Special* you may just want to fold a smaller-sized hat from notebook paper or typing paper. Sometimes it's easier to make a small hat first (as practice) and then do the full-sized model.

First turn your double page of newspaper (or sheet of notebook paper) into a square. Fold one corner over, so that the sheet of paper looks like the first illustration.

Once this is done, cut off the part of the paper shown by the shaded area in Illus. 2. When you unfold the paper you'll have a perfectly square piece of material remaining.

Remember how to make a square sheet of paper from a rectangle because you'll need to do this for some other toys in this book.

Now, let's get going on the *Viking Special*. Fold one corner of the paper over so it looks like Illus. 3. Since you already have a diagonal fold (from making the sheet of paper square), just refold the paper along that diagonal. The two dotted lines in the drawing indicate where you'll be making your next folds.

Fold the two upper corners down along the dotted lines shown in Illus. 3. Make certain the pointed corners you fold down come exactly together as shown in Illus. 4.

Of course, the two dotted lines in Illus. 4 show where to make the next folds. But wait! Don't fold yet. These next folds will involve just the top layer of paper (You folded this layer down a few seconds ago.) Don't try to fold all the layers

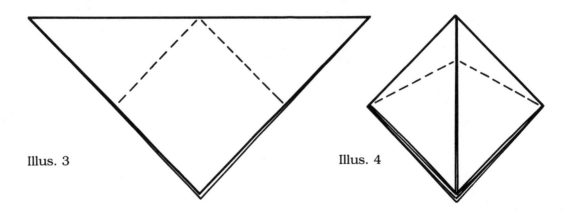

Illus. 3                    Illus. 4

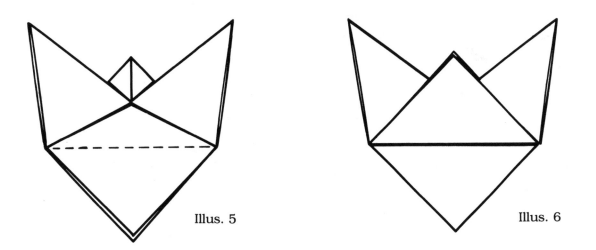

Illus. 5

Illus. 6

of paper, because you can't. (If you could, it would ruin the *Viking Special*.)

Check Illus. 5 to see how the *Viking Special* looks after you've made these two folds.

Once again, the dotted line in the drawing in Illus. 5 shows the next fold. Once again, this fold involves only the top layer of paper. Don't fold both layers.

When you've folded the top layer of paper along the dotted line, your *Viking Special* is shown in Illus. 6.

Turn the hat over so it looks like the one in Illus. 7.

Make the two folds along the dotted lines shown in Illus. 7.

Once these folds are finished your *Viking Special* will be almost ready to wear. If looks just like the one shown in Illus. 8.

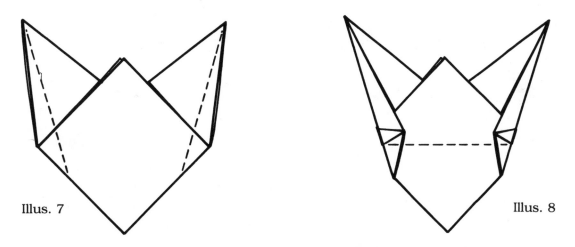

Illus. 7

Illus. 8

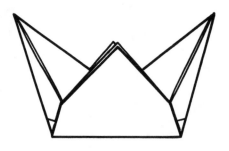

Just fold up the bottom along the dotted line and you've reached the final stage shown in Illus. 9.

Open the bottom of the hat and it should fit your head nicely. Of course, if you made a model from notebook paper, the hat will fit a doll's head, instead of your own head.

For a great party hat, or just to brighten up the finished project, you can also use plain white paper, or brown butcher paper or craft paper, and paint or color the hat with any designs you wish.

Now that you're a skilled hat maker, let's take a look at another terrific paper hat.

Don't you just love my new hat?

# Multipurpose Cap

This cap will take only a minute to make, and it can be used for a variety of purposes. It looks very much like the cloth hat worn by members of the armed services. Use white shelving paper and put a red cross on it and you'll have a perfect nurse's cap.

Make this cap from newspaper to keep the dust out of your hair the next time you have to clean the garage or the basement. For that matter, use white shelving paper, color it with your school team's colors, and then wear it on school spirit day or to athletic events.

Use gift-wrapping paper and then wear it as a party hat or as a hat for special holidays.

Begin with a square sheet of paper. (Remember how to make a square from a rectangular sheet of paper? Check Illus. 1 and 2 if you've forgotten.)

Even if you want to make this quick cap using white shelving paper, it's a good idea to make the first model from a full sheet of newspaper. You can check for size without using up your gift-wrapping or shelf paper.

Can't you wait until I've finished?

Fold the square of paper in half so it looks like Illus. 10. The dotted line in the drawing shows where you'll be making the next fold.

As soon as you make this second fold, the hat will look like Illus. 11. At this point, your paper is four layers thick.

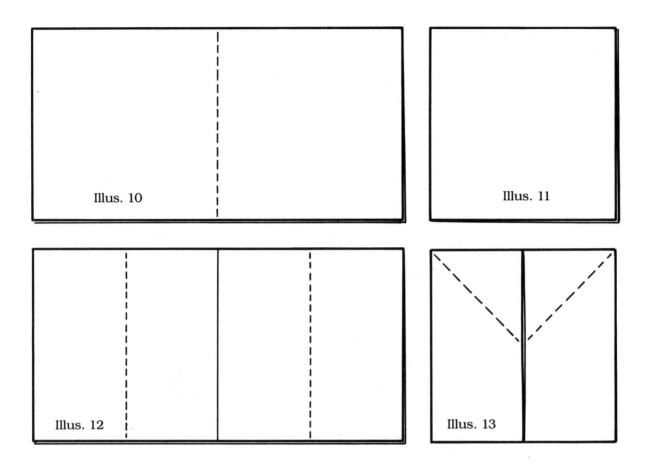

Illus. 10

Illus. 11

Illus. 12

Illus. 13

Unfold the last fold so your hat-to-be looks like Illus. 12. Then fold each side in towards the middle fold. The two dotted lines in the drawing show where to make these folds.

After folding both sides in to the middle, fold your *Multi-purpose Cap* as shown in Illus. 13. The two dotted lines tell you where you'll be making your next folds. Fold the top

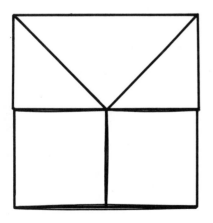

Illus. 14

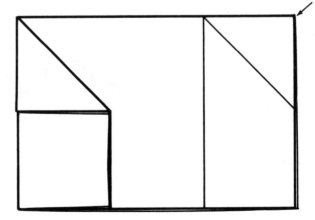

Illus. 15

layer only. Once you make these folds, your project is shown in Illus. 14.

Now comes the tricky part. It's not all that difficult to accomplish the next few steps, but you do have to pay attention.

Unfold the right-hand of the project so it looks like the drawing in Illus. 15. Push in at the point shown by the arrow.

As you push in on the upper right-hand corner, the fold will turn inside out and you'll end up with what you see in

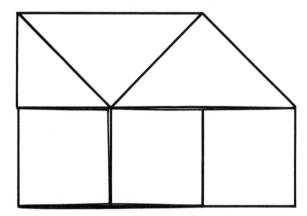

Illus. 16

Illus. 16. The right-hand side of the cap looks like the flattened end of a house, doesn't it?

Now do the same thing for the left side of the cap and your project will look just like the drawing in Illus. 17.

The dotted lines in Illus. 17 indicate your next folds. These folds have to be made so that the ends are folded under the rest of the cap.

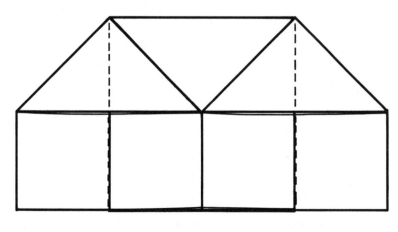

Illus. 17

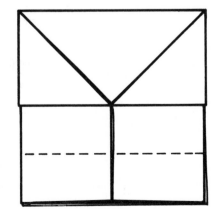

Illus. 18

15

Once you fold both ends back and under the cap, things look like Illus. 18.

Before you start folding on the dotted line in Illus. 18, you need to know that you will fold only the top section of paper. Separate the top two layers of paper from the bottom two layers and fold only these top layers.

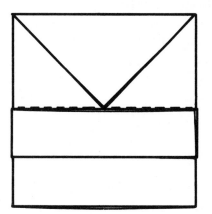

Illus. 19

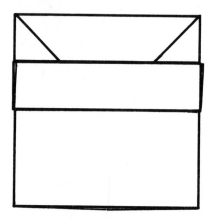

Illus. 20

Fold the paper up along the dotted line, and you're at Illus. 19. The dotted line in the drawing shows you are going to make another fold.

Once you've made the next fold your *Multipurpose Cap* is shown in Illus. 20.

Turn the cap over, and then fold the bottom up in two folds just like you did on the front side. When these folds are made, your all-purpose headgear is finished. (See Illus. 21.)

Open the bottom of the cap, and it's ready to wear. Once it is open, the folded flaps on either side will stay in place. You can use a short piece of tape wrapped around each end of the cap to keep these flaps in place even when the hat isn't on your head. The tape is seen in Illus. 21. Decorate it, if you wish, or wear it just as it is.

Illus. 21

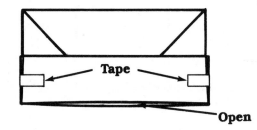

Tape

Open

# Printing Press Special

We don't think of paper hats as being famous, but here's one that is. There isn't any doubt that more *Printing Press Specials* have been folded and worn than any other kind of paper hat.

The people who ran newspaper printing presses began folding and wearing this hat to keep bits of ink, dust, and paper lint out of their hair. It became a tradition for those operating printing presses to grab a piece of newspaper and fold a hat before starting work each day.

Even if you aren't in the printing business, you can wear your *Printing Press Special* as a work hat, or just to let people know that you, too, have learned how to make this famous piece of headgear.

Begin with a double page from a full-sized newspaper. It is already folded, so you are working with two layers of paper. Place the fold away from you on your desk or table (just like the drawing in Illus. 22). Make the two folds shown (dotted lines) in the drawing.

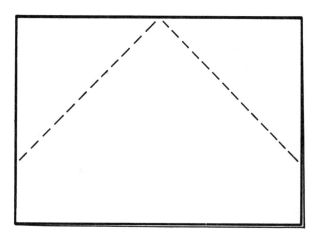

Illus. 22

Once these folds are made, your *Printing Press Special* will look like Illus. 23.

Next fold only the top layer of paper up along the dotted line seen in Illus. 23. When this fold is made your hat has moved along to Illus. 24

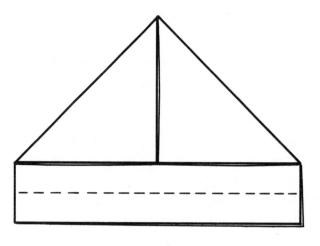

Illus. 23

Make your next fold along the dotted line in Illus. 24. You're still folding just the top layer of newspaper.

When this fold is in place, you have reached Illus. 25. Now, turn the paper over so it looks like Illus. 26.

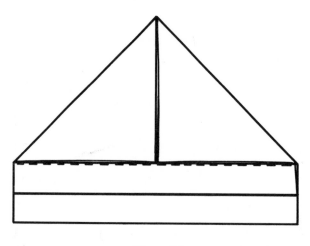

Illus. 24

The two dotted lines in Illus. 26 are your next folds. Before you make these folds, try to judge how large you want this hat to be. You'll want it to fit your head perfectly. What you want now is to leave enough space between the two folds in Illus. 26 so the hat will be an exact fit. Don't worry if your first hat is a bit large or a little small. You can adjust the size by refolding it, or just by making a new one. The great thing

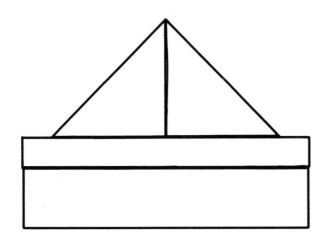

Illus. 25

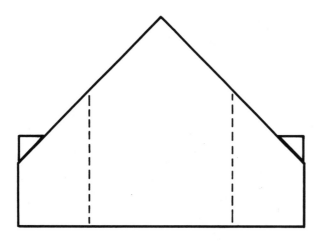

Illus. 26

is that you can make the *Printing Press Special* larger or smaller just by changing the space between this pair of folds. When these folds are in place, your hat will look like Illus. 27.

Fold the bottom corners up along the dotted lines shown in Illus. 27. With these folds in place, that hat is shown in Illus. 28. Check the two dotted lines in Illus. 28. These are your next folds.

Fold the bottom up and crease the first fold. Then fold the bottom up again so that your hat looks like Illus. 29.

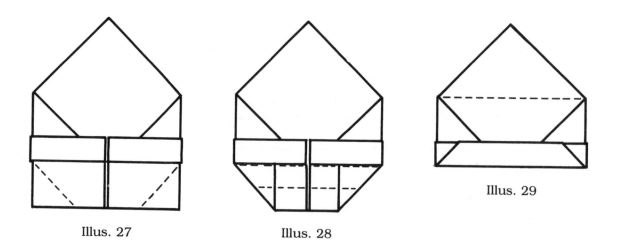

Illus. 27

Illus. 28

Illus. 29

Check the dotted line in Illus. 29. When you fold the pointed top of the hat towards you, fold it down far enough so you can tuck the point under the flap you made when you folded the bottom of the hat *up* in the last step.

When you finish this step, your hat looks like Illus. 30. You'll have to hold the bottom flap in place for just a minute, or the top point will try to slip out from under the flap.

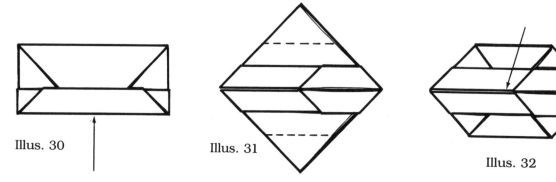

Illus. 30

Illus. 31

Illus. 32

Here's the hardest step in making your *Printing Press Special*. You are already holding the flap and the tucked-in point (with one hand) at the spot shown by the arrow in Illus. 30. Keep a firm grip on that side of the hat with one hand. Take hold of the opposite side of the hat with your other hand.

Now turn the hat over so you are looking at the bottom of the hat. Pull your hands apart slowly but firmly. This will cause the open part of the hat to close up as both ends pull in together. Carefully press the ends down so that the hat flattens out and looks like Illus. 31.

You are now looking at the *bottom* of the hat. The top is flat on the table or desk. There are two dotted lines for new folds in Illus. 31. When you folded the pointed top down you folded it so that the point fit under the flap at the bottom of the hat. You're going to do exactly the same sort of folding job again.

Fold each pointed end over, so that the point can tuck under the flap. Once both these folds are in place, and the points securely tucked under the flaps, your *Printing Press Special* will look like Illus. 32.

Open up the hat by inserting your thumbs at the point shown by the arrow. Gently pull the sides of the hat apart. You have a genuine model of the most often folded and worn paper hat in history.

If you misjudged the size and your hat is a bit loose or too snug, either refold it now or fold a new one. There's no need to settle for anything other than perfection with this great paper hat.

You know you can adjust it to fit right!

## Turkish Fez

This terrific paper hat can be folded in just a matter of seconds—once you've made your first one. If you have some stuffed animals in need of hats, the *Turkish Fez* should fill the bill.

Start this paper hat with a square piece of paper. If you need to review the process, Illus. 1 and 2 show how to square a sheet of paper. If you're making the *Turkish Fez* for a stuffed animal or doll, a sheet of notebook or typing paper should be about the right size. If you're making a *Fez* for yourself, use a sheet of paper about the size of a large double sheet of newspaper.

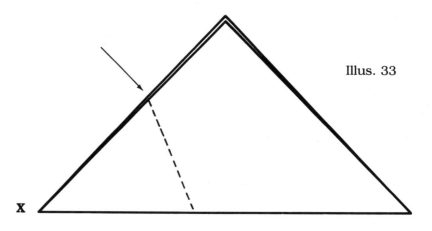

Illus. 33

Fold the square in half so that it looks like Illus. 33. Since you made a diagonal fold when you squared your paper, this step is a snap—just refold it along the diagonal fold.

The dotted line in Illus. 33 shows your first fold. Everything about making the *Fez* correctly depends on getting the first fold exactly right.

The arrow in the drawing indicates the key point when making this first fold. It is just a little more than halfway up from the bottom point towards the top point of the paper. With this as a clue, take hold of the bottom point which is marked with an "X." Bend it along the dotted line but don't crease the fold just yet.

Look at Illus. 34 before completing this first fold. See how the fold is located so that the tip of the bottom corner just reaches the opposite side of the paper. Note also that the folded edge of the paper is now parallel with the base of the paper.

Once you have the fold bent into place so it is exactly like Illus. 34, go ahead and crease the fold. At this point, con-

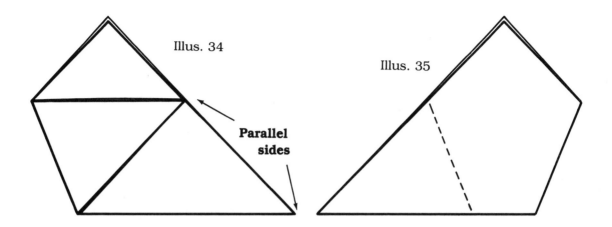

Illus. 34

**Parallel sides**

Illus. 35

gratulate yourself. The only difficult part of making a *Turkish Fez* is now behind you.

Turn the *Fez* over so that it looks like Illus. 35. The dotted line in the drawing shows your next fold.

When you make this fold, just be sure this side of the *Fez* matches the opposite side. This is easy. The arrow in Illus. 36 shows where the top of the folded section on the other side is located. Begin your new fold exactly where that tip of paper touches the other side of the hat. When you do this, the side you're working on now will come out parallel to the base, just as the first side did in Illus. 34.

Your *Fez* appears at this stage in Illus. 37. The dotted line shows the next fold to be made. Fold only the top layer of paper towards you. Tuck it into the inside of the section you just folded over.

Illus. 38 shows the *Fez* with the fold completed and tucked away out of sight.

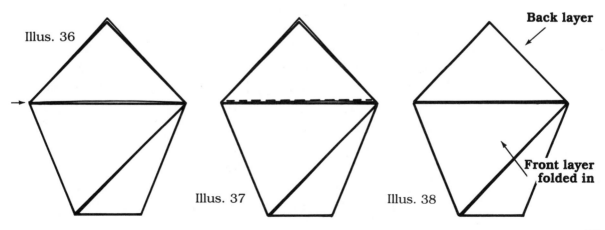

Illus. 36

Illus. 37

Illus. 38

**Back layer**

**Front layer folded in**

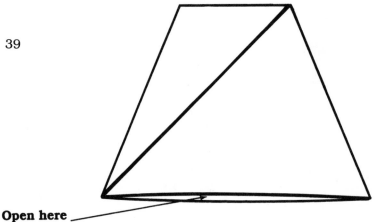

**Open here**

Now turn the hat over and fold the remaining layer of paper down and tuck it away, just as you did a minute ago with the other side of the hat. Your *Turkish Fez* now looks just like the one in Illus. 39.

If you made the *Fez* from white or plain paper, consider decorating it with colored crayons or paints. Stickers are a quick way to decorate any paper hat you make.

This is a quick party hat you can make with wrapping paper in just a few seconds. The *Fez* is a good hat for those times you just feel like making a terrific paper hat quickly and easily.

## Let's Have a Party Hat

Paper hats and parties seem to go together. Here's a party hat that is just a little bit fancy yet it's simple to fold quickly. It's also another good hat for your stuffed animals or other toys who need some different headgear.

If the *Let's Have a Party Hat* is for you, you'll need a piece of material about the size of a large sheet of newspaper. Plain paper is good if you're going to decorate it with designs or stickers. Wrapping paper with a holiday or special design is perfect for those occasions. Newspaper makes a terrific paper hat any day of the year. The choice is yours.

You'll need a square piece of paper for your *Let's Have a Party Hat*. Fold it in the middle so it looks like Illus. 40.

The dotted line in Illus. 40 shows your next fold. Fold up only the top layer of paper when making this fold.

Illus. 41 shows your hat after this fold. Now fold the paper in half along the dotted line you see in the drawing.

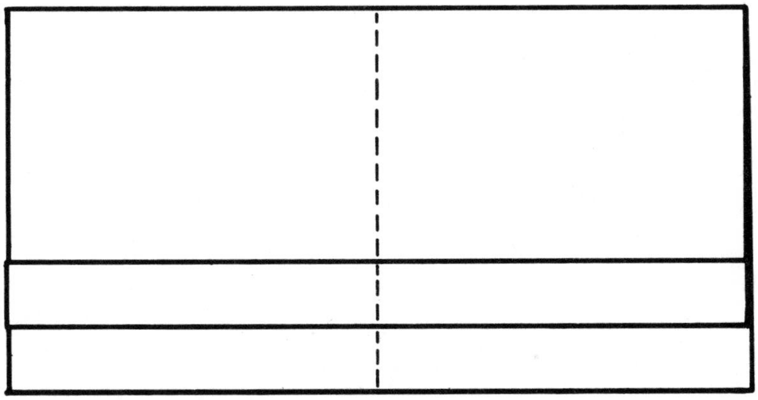

Illus. 41

Once you've folded the paper in half, unfold it and turn the paper over. What you see before you on your desk or table should look just like Illus. 42. The fold you just made forms a little mountain in the middle of the sheet of paper.

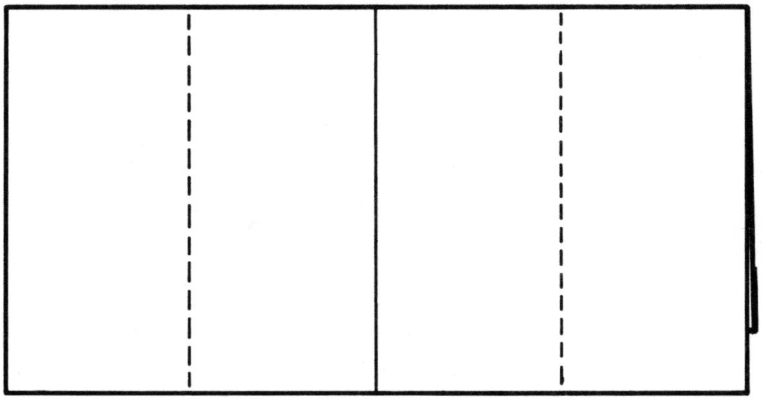

Illus. 42

25

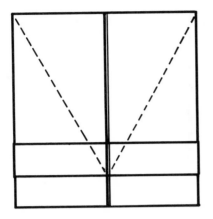

Illus. 43

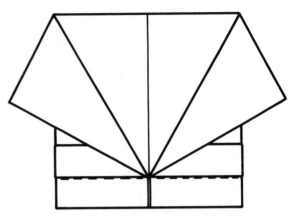

Illus. 44

Fold both sides along the dotted lines in Illus. 42. Make certain each side comes right to the middle fold. When these folds are in place, your hat should look like Illus. 43.

The two dotted lines in Illus. 43 represent the next pair of folds you'll be making. When you make these folds, be sure that they run from the upper corner right down to the bottom edge of the folded border. Check the dotted lines in the drawing to make certain you have these folds located correctly.

Once these folds are made, you'll end up with points of paper extending beyond the rest of the hat. This is the way the *Let's Have a Party Hat* is supposed to look. After all, a party hat needs to have a few fancy points to it.

With this pair of folds in place your hat should look a lot like the drawing in Illus. 44.

Fold the bottom of the hat up along the dotted line (shown in Illus. 44) and your hat is ready to try on. The finished hat is seen in Illus. 45.

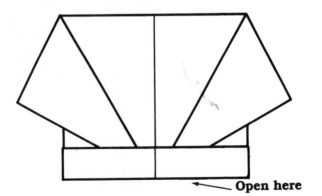

Illus. 45

⟵ **Open here**

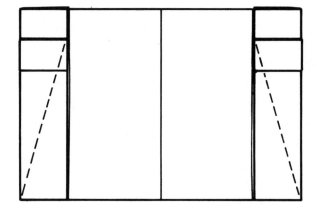

Illus. 46

You can decorate this hat using paints, crayons, or stickers. If you made it using wrapping paper, it's already decorated. Either way, all you need now is a party so you can wear your hat. If you don't have a party handy, wear it anyhow. There's something about wearing a terrific new paper hat which brightens up almost any day.

Now that you know how to fold this party hat, let's go back to Illus. 42 (page 25) for just a minute. You folded both sides right to the middle fold. How about making a little change at this point, and giving your next *Let's Have a Party Hat* a different look?

Begin a new party hat just as you did in Illus. 40 and 41 (page 25). When you reach Illus. 42, don't fold the sides to the center fold. Instead, fold them in only halfway or so. Illus. 46 shows how your changed party hat looks now.

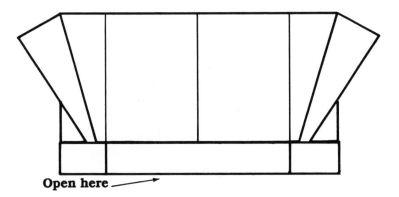

**Open here** ⟶

Illus. 47

Finish the hat just as you did before. When the final fold is made, your new and improved model looks like the one shown in Illus. 47.

Not only does this folding change add variety, but it also lets you make this hat fit your head exactly. You can check your head size when you make the folds shown in Illus. 46 and locate the folds so the completed party hat is a perfect fit. Give it a try and see for yourself.

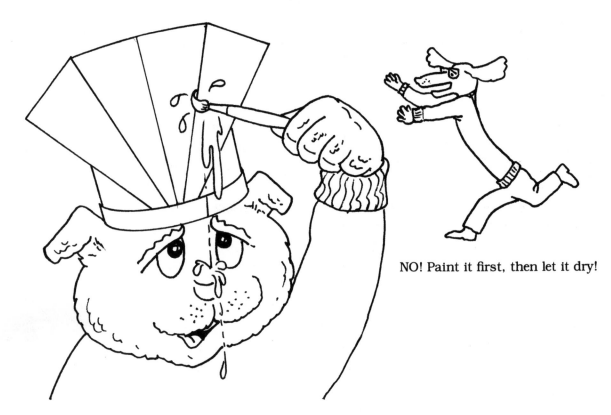

NO! Paint it first, then let it dry!

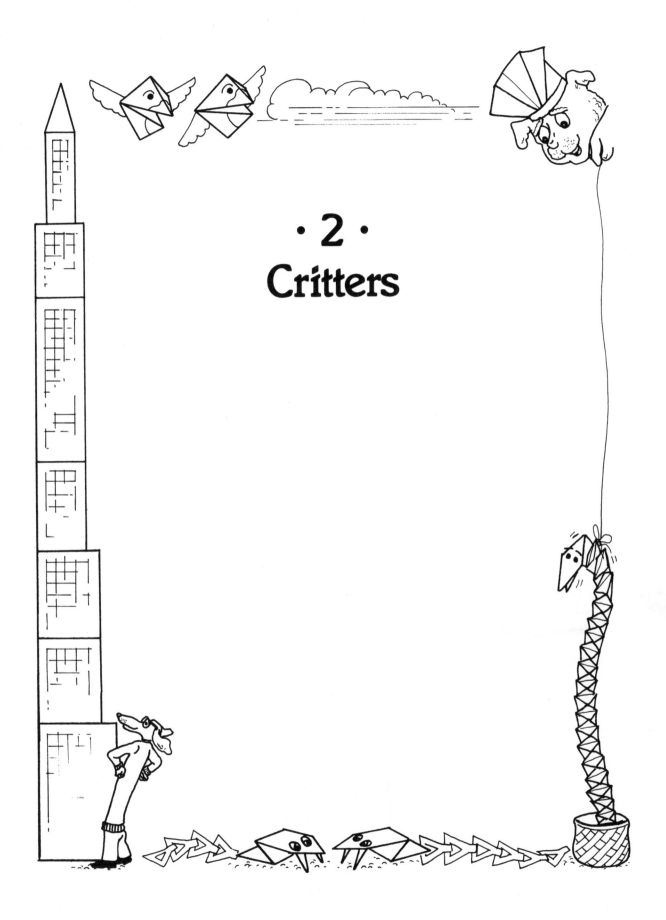

# · 2 ·
# Critters

# CRITTERS

The terrific paper toys in this chapter are all somewhat like animals. They behave like slinky snakes, or their jaws can pick up small items. Their legs move, or their mouths open and close at your command.

Since most of these paper toys aren't *animal* toys we'll call them *Critters*. A *Critter* can be almost anything you want it to be.

## Slinky Snake

This paper toy is extremely easy to make, even if it does take a few minutes of work. Once your *Slinky Snake* is finished it's great for entertaining small children, it's fun to carry around and make it slink, or it can be used as a room decoration.

If you have colored paper available, you can make your *Slinky Snake* from green paper or perhaps yellow or brown. If you don't have any colored paper, white notebook or typing paper and a couple of crayons will work just fine.

Your *Slinky Snake* is made from strips of paper about three-fourths of an inch wide and cut as long as the sheet of paper. If you're using white paper and crayons, color the paper before you begin cutting it into strips. A good way to do this is to make a strip of green color one-fourth of an inch (or so) wide. Add a similar strip of yellow or brown next to the green. (If you wish, your *Slinky Snake* can be red or orange or any other color. That's up to you. After all, it's your critter.)

Continue coloring by alternating bands of color until you have colored three (or so) inches of your paper. How much paper you need to color depends upon how long your *Slinky Snake* is going to be. Let's start making your first *Slinky Snake* and then *you* can decide how long it will be.

Cut two strips of paper three-fourths of an inch wide. Use a bit of cellophane tape or a drop of glue to fasten the ends together so the two strips are at right angles. Illus. 48 shows how.

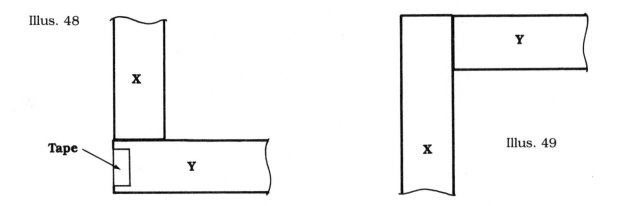

Illus. 48

Tape

X

Y

Y

X

Illus. 49

You will fold these strips over each other to make what some people call a "cat spring." It's easy to do, but it does take a little bit of time. Begin by folding the strip marked with the "X" in Illus. 48 over the top of the other strip. Once this is done, your *Slinky Snake* is shown in Illus. 49.

Now fold strip "Y" over the top of the strip you just folded over. Once this is done, you've reached Illus. 50.

Keep alternating this folding process until you've used most of both strips. Then use either tape or glue to attach the next strips you cut to the ends of the strips you've been folding. Tape is better for this than glue, since you have to allow some time to let the glue dry.

If you wish, it's fine to tape two strips together (to begin with), and then to add strips two at a time. Don't try to tape too many strips together all at once. If you do, you'll find yourself all tangled up as you fold the strips back and forth over each other.

You can put a bit of extra curve and twist into your *Slinky Snake* if you don't make all the folds square. Illus. 51 shows

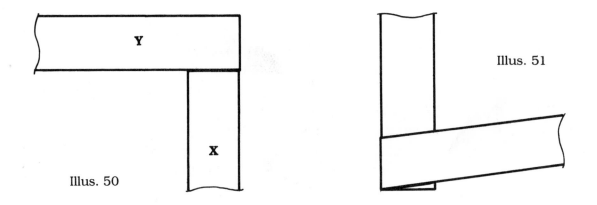

Y

X

Illus. 50

Illus. 51

how to make a fold at just a bit of an angle. This causes your "cat spring" to begin to turn and take on a little twist. By putting an angle fold every three or four folds, your snake will twist and turn a bit.

By now, you're probably amazed to see how many strips of paper it takes to construct a long *Slinky Snake*. If you're coloring your paper strips, you'll have to take a minute or two to add more color, since you've used up all the paper you colored in order to begin this project.

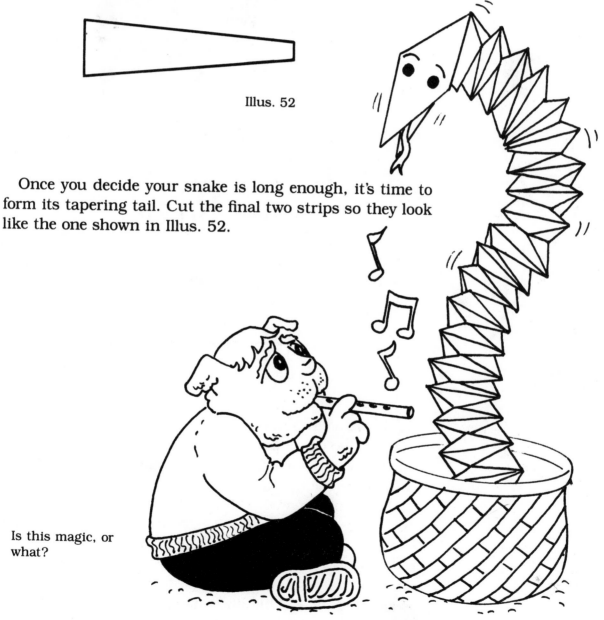

Illus. 52

Once you decide your snake is long enough, it's time to form its tapering tail. Cut the final two strips so they look like the one shown in Illus. 52.

Is this magic, or what?

The last strips should be three-fourths inch wide at the wider end and taper down to one-fourth inch at the thin end. This gives your snake's tail a nicely tapered end. You could make one pair of strips from three-fourths to one-half inch and a second pair which begins at one-half inch and tapers to one-fourth inch. That way you have a longer tail.

When you finally reach the end of the tail after about a million folds just use a bit of tape or glue to fasten the loose ends together. If one end is longer than the other just let it stick out. It makes a perfect tail tip.

Illus. 53 shows two ideas for making your *Slinky Snake's* head. Just cut the diamond out of paper or perhaps a file card and make it only a little wider than the body of the snake.

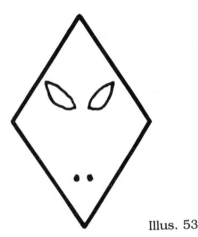 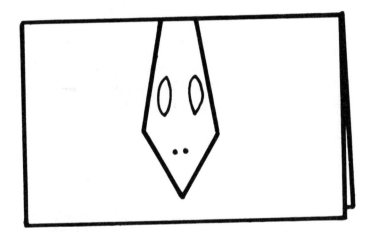

Illus. 53

Illus. 53 also shows how to make a different sort of head. Just fold a piece of paper or even a file card in half and cut out the head. Glue or tape the bottom section to the body. This allows the mouth to open and close. If you wish, color the inside of the mouth red.

By the way, it takes about eight to ten pairs of strips to construct a *Slinky Snake* two feet long. Right. *Now* we tell you!

If you wish, you can make some strips in the middle of the snake a bit wider. This gives its body thickness. If you do this just remember to start the first of these strips the same width (three-fourths inch) as the first strips. Then taper the body strips (just like you did the tail), except now the strips get wider. The next strips start wide to match the width you ended with. When you have enough body thickness, start tapering the strips back to normal width.

You can make *Slinky Snakes* thicker or thinner than the one you just did. They can be as long or as short as you want them to be. Once you're through playing with this critter, you can coil it on a shelf or let it wrap itself around an item in your room.

# Fun-Time Puppet

Here's your chance to make good use of an empty cereal box or the box your dog's biscuits came in. Turn that empty box into a terrific *Fun-Time Puppet* with arms that wave and legs that kick.

Begin by cutting the top out of the empty box completely. Once this is done, turn the box over so that the open end becomes the bottom of your puppet-to-be.

Instead of using a cereal box, you could use a half-gallon milk carton or a juice carton. If you do this, you'll need to rinse the carton carefully, because you don't want stale milk or sticky juice running down the insides of your puppet and then onto your hand and arm.

First cover the front of the box or carton with white paper so that you can design a face for your puppet without having the puppet look like an ordinary cereal box with two eyes and a mouth.

Spread some glue or paste on the front of the box and just press the paper into place. With some milk or juice cartons this doesn't work too well because the cartons are slick; certain kinds of glue and paste don't hold well. Another way to attach paper to the front of your box or carton is to use tape. Cellophane tape or masking tape both work. When using tape, fold the paper over so that it extends down each side of the box. The tape will be out of sight when someone looks your puppet in the eye.

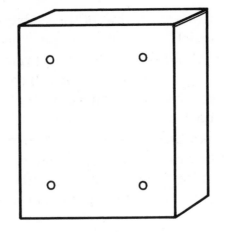

The hardest part of making this *Fun-Time Puppet* is attaching its arms and legs, so let's get that part out of the way first. Turn the puppet over—you're looking at the back of the box. Decide how high you want the arms and legs on your puppet. Poke one hole in the back of the box for each arm and each leg. Locate these holes about one inch from each side of the box. Illus. 54 shows these holes in place.

Watch that point, friend! That's a tool, not a toy!

The point of a ballpoint pen is perfect for poking these holes. If you use something else, such as scissors, just don't poke your finger. The four holes don't have to be very big. All that will go through them is either a paper fastener or one side of a paper clip.

Let's make the arms and legs. They don't have to be fancy. After all, an empty cereal box (or an empty milk carton) isn't all that fancy! For your first *Fun-Time Puppet* keep the arms and legs basic and simple. You can get artistic with your next puppet—after you see how this one works.

Illus. 55 shows a simple arm and a simple leg for a puppet. This puppet critter some may think of as a bear and others may see just as a critter.

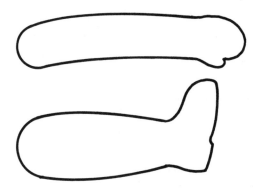

Illus. 55

Since the arms and legs need to be stiff, cut them out of cereal-box material. Since they are going to be connected to the back of the box, make the arms and legs long enough to stick out past the edge of the box.

Draw one arm and one leg and then cut them out. Use the ones you just cut out as patterns for the second arm and the second leg so you end up with two identical arms and legs.

If you have a hole punch here's a good time to use it. Make two holes in each arm and each leg as shown in Illus. 56. Be

Illus. 56

sure the hole nearer to the end of the arm or leg is at least one-half inch from the end of the material. Otherwise, the material may tear when you put your puppet through its paces.

When no hole punch is handy, use a ballpoint pen or the point of your scissors to make these holes. Place the material on a thick pad of newspaper so that you poke the holes through the cardboard and into the newspaper. Don't get a finger in the way—and don't poke holes in your desk or table!

The control piece will let you move the arms and legs of your finished puppet. This piece needs to be of stiff cardboard. A good way to make the control piece is to cut a piece of cereal-box cardboard two and one-half inches wide and as long as the cereal box is tall. Fold that piece of cardboard in half down the middle and glue or tape it together. This gives you a stiff control piece about one and one-quarter inches wide.

Place your control piece beside one of the pairs of holes you poked in the back of the cereal box. Illus. 57 shows this

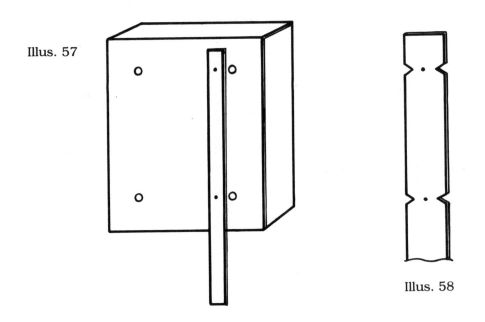

Illus. 57

Illus. 58

step. Use your pen or pencil to mark and transfer the locations of the holes in the box onto the control piece. The dots in Illus. 57 show these locations.

Now carefully cut a little wedge of material out of each side of the control piece opposite each of the two dots you just made. Check Illus. 58 to see how the control piece looks with these wedges cut out.

Now comes the fun! Cut two pieces of string so each piece is about eighteen inches long. You'll use this string to connect the arms and legs to the control piece.

Tie one end of the string to one of the arms as shown in Illus. 59. Be sure you tie the string into the hole nearest the

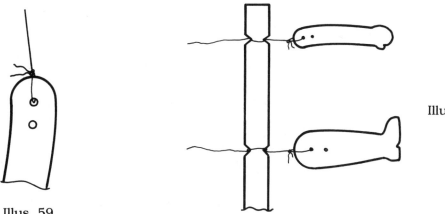

Illus. 60

Illus. 59

end of the arm. Wrap the string one time around the control piece so the string fits into the wedges you cut. Do not tie the string to the control piece. It has to remain loose so you can adjust it—this step is coming soon.

Do the same thing for one of the legs as you did for one of the arms. Illus. 60 shows your progress.

Now it's time to fasten the arm and leg to the holes you already poked in the box. If you have *paper fasteners*, they will make the fastening easy. Just put a fastener through the second (outer) hole in one of the arms, push the prongs through the hole in the box, and then reach inside the box and flatten out the fastener's prongs.

Don't worry if you can't find any paper fasteners; you can use paper clips instead. Illus. 61 shows how a paper clip is used to attach one of the arms to the box.

The main part of the paper clip is inside the box. Slip the loose end of the clip through the hole in the box. Then slide

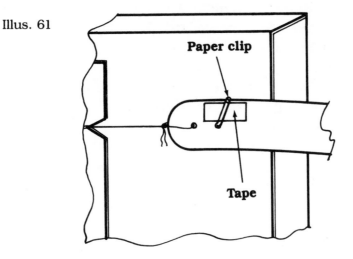

**Paper clip**

**Tape**

it through the hole in the puppet's arm. Once this is done, press a strip of tape over the paper clip, as shown in Illus. 61. This is necessary to keep the puppet's arm from sliding off the paper clip when the arm begins to wave.

Fasten the puppet's leg to the box just as you did its arm. With this done, it's adjustment time.

Loosen or tighten the string looped around the control piece so that the control strip is right in the middle of the box. Illus. 62 shows how it should look.

When you have the control piece centered, wrap the string around it one more time. Now attach the second arm and the second leg to the control strip. Make sure the holes in the

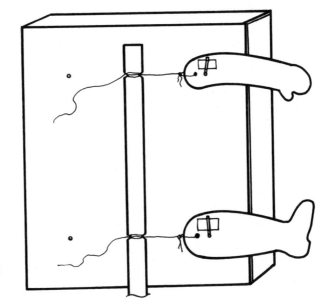

Illus. 62

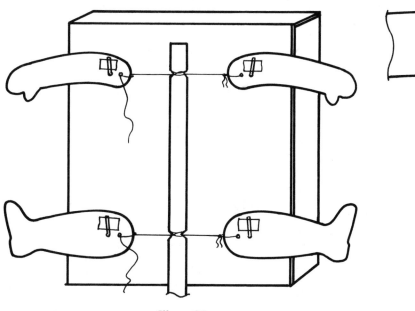

Illus. 63

**Tape**

Illus. 64

arms and the legs line up with the holes you already punched in the box. This step is shown in Illus. 63.

After you have your spacing right, push the string through the hole in the arm and leg again. This gives you two wraps of string around the end of the arms and legs. Why? Because you aren't going to tie a knot in the string just yet, and you don't want the string to slide back and forth.

Illus. 64 gives you an idea how the end of one of the arms looks with the string going through the hole twice.

Run the loose end of the string around the control piece two or three times. Instead of worrying about trying to tie a knot somewhere, just use a piece of tape to hold the loose end of the string in place. Illus. 65 shows how.

Illus. 65

Attach the legs just as you did the arms. Fasten both the arms and legs to the box using paper fasteners or paper clips and your *Fun-Time Puppet* is ready to kick its legs and wave its arms. Just move the control piece up and down and the arms and legs will move with it.

What's a puppet without eyes? Turn the box over so that the white paper faces up. You can use crayons, felt-tipped markers, or paints to give color to the puppet's eyes, nose

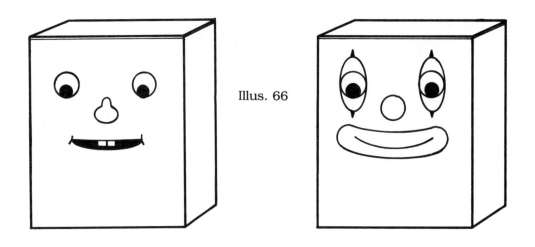

Illus. 66

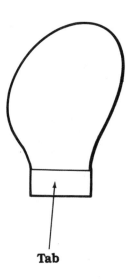

Illus. 67

**Tab**

and mouth. Or, you can cut out these items from colored paper.

Illus. 66 gives two ideas for puppet faces. You could cut out the various parts of the eyes from papers of different colors. Otherwise, paint or color them on the front of the puppet.

Cut out the ears from colored paper or color them on stiff paper and then cut them out. Leave a little tab at the bottom of each ear so it can slip between the box and the paper. Illus. 67 shows how to make the tab. Use tape or glue to fasten the ears in place. Illus. 68 shows one pair of ears in place.

Another way to attach the ears is to fold back the tab at the bottom of the ear, and then you can glue or tape the ear onto the top or the side of the box.

Let your imagination work for you and remember that critters don't have to look like any *real* animal. If you want, make your next *Fun-Time Puppet* look like a clown. You can give it a funny hat and attach the ears to the sides of the box rather than to the top.

Small cardboard boxes (such as those used for macaroni-and-cheese meals) or quart (litre) milk cartons make terrific *Fun-Time Puppets*, but they're a bit harder to work with than the larger boxes.

What if you want the arms and legs to be on the *front* of the box? Can this be done? It can, but it takes more work.

If you decide to put the arms and legs on the front of the box, the control piece has to go *inside* the box. This calls for two changes. First, make *six* holes in the front of the box

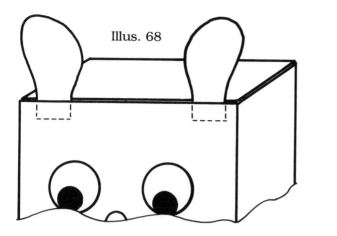

Illus. 68

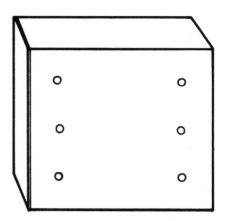

Illus. 69

instead of the four you'd make in the back. Illus. 69 shows how to arrange these holes.

Second, wrap the strings around the control piece as your first step when attaching the arms and leg. Wrap each string around the strip three or four times, then tie the string right in the middle of the strip. Illus. 70 shows how this is done.

Place the control strip *inside* the box and run both ends of the strings out the extra middle row of holes you made. Attach the strings to the arms and legs and tie each end of the string to each arm and each leg. Pull the string tight so the control strip comes right to the front of the box and there isn't a lot of slack in the string.

This is harder than putting the arms and legs on the back of the box, but you can do it if you just have a little patience. Borrow an extra pair of hands to help hold things.

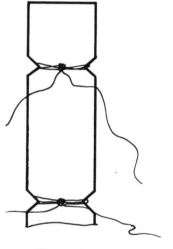

Illus. 70

## Cat's Meow

People used to say that something terrific was the *Cat's Meow*. Here's a folded cat's face you can use as a talking-head puppet. It only takes a minute or two to make. You'll use notebook paper or typing paper.

Begin with a square piece of notebook paper or typing paper. Illus. 1 and 2 on page 9 show how to turn a rectangle of paper into a square.

Start by folding one corner over to the opposite corner to give you a center fold. Illus. 71 shows this step. You probably

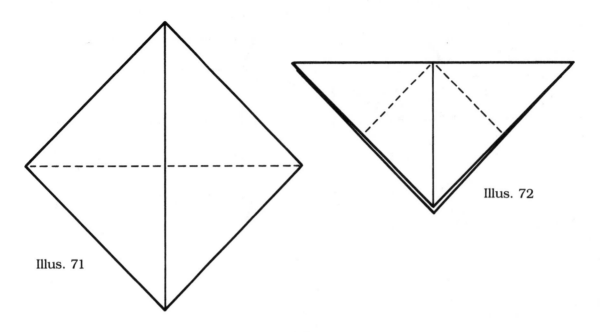

Illus. 71

Illus. 72

already accomplished this step when you squared your paper.

Unfold the paper. Now fold your paper down along the dotted line in Illus. 71. Once this is done, your project looks like Illus. 72.

Your next two folds are shown by the dotted lines in Illus. 72. Fold each corner down to the bottom corner and crease the folds.

Once these two folds have been made and creased, unfold the paper so that it looks like Illus. 73.

The pair of dotted lines shown in Illus. 73 show where to make your next two folds.

Fold both corners over so that they meet at the middle fold. Once these folds are made, your *Cat's Meow* looks like Illus. 74.

Now turn the paper over. It should look like Illus. 75.

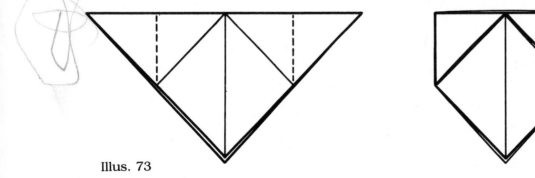

Illus. 73

Illus. 74

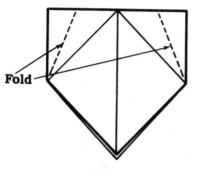

Illus. 75

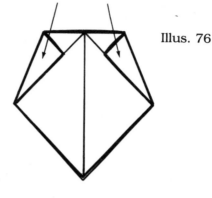

Illus. 76

Make the two folds indicated by the pair of dotted lines in Illus. 75. Fold each corner over so that each corner just reaches the crease already in the paper.

The next drawing, Illus. 76, shows how things look after these folds are in place.

Once these two folds are made, open out the triangular flaps from behind the cat's head. The arrows in Illus. 76 show the hidden points of these flaps behind the rest of the project.

Illus. 77 shows the ears in place. The dotted line in the drawing tells where to make your next fold. This fold will be only for the top layer of paper.

Fold the top layer of paper under and tuck it up between the two layers of paper. What you're folding now is the mouth of your *Cat's Meow*.

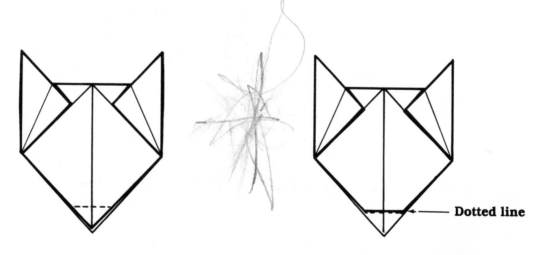

Illus. 77

Illus. 78

Dotted line

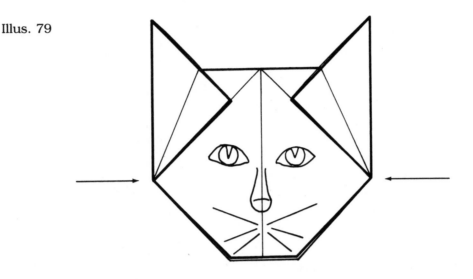

Illus. 79

In Illus. 78 you see the top layer folded into the cat's mouth. The dotted line shows that you're going to fold the bottom layer just like you did the top layer. This time fold the paper up so that you can tuck the bottom layer of paper into the mouth, as well.

Now it's time for a bit of quick art work. Check Illus. 79 to see how you can add eyes, whiskers, and a nose to your *Cat's Meow* to make your moving cat mask look even more like a cat. Use crayons, felt-tipped markers, pencil, or pen to add these markings.

The two arrows show where to press in on the sides to make your *Cat's Meow* open its mouth as its face moves forward and backwards.

If you wish (and you probably will), color the bottom flap inside the mouth pink or red to give your *Cat's Meow* a tongue—you'll see it when you press in on the sides of the mask.

## Gabby

*Gabby* is a paper head—it opens and closes its beak at your command. *Gabby* is strong enough to pick up objects in its beak—pencils, pens, and the like.

Begin by cutting a sheet of notebook paper or typing paper so that it's six inches wide and seven inches long. After

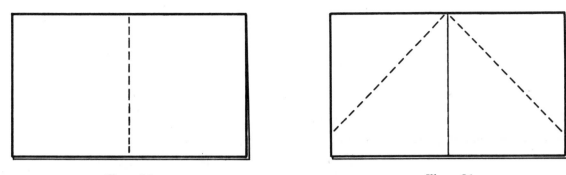

Illus. 80

Illus. 81

you make your first *Gabby* you can make others larger or smaller (if you wish) just by changing the size of your paper.

Place the paper in front of you so the six-inch side is facing you. Fold the paper down and in half so your project looks like Illus. 80.

Fold the paper in half along the dotted line in Illus. 80. Then unfold it. That fold was just to give us a middle crease—it's shown in Illus. 81.

The pair of dotted lines in Illus. 81 indicate your next two folds. Fold the corners right to the middle crease you just made. When these folds are in place, your *Gabby* will look like Illus. 82.

The next fold you need to make is along the dotted line seen in Illus. 82. Fold only the top layer of paper up when you make this fold. Illus. 83 shows the project with this fold made.

Turn *Gabby* over and fold the other side up so it matches the fold you just made. Your project now looks like Illus. 84.

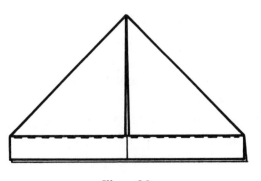

Illus. 82

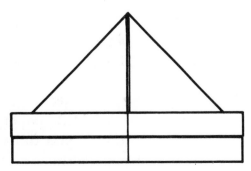

Illus. 83

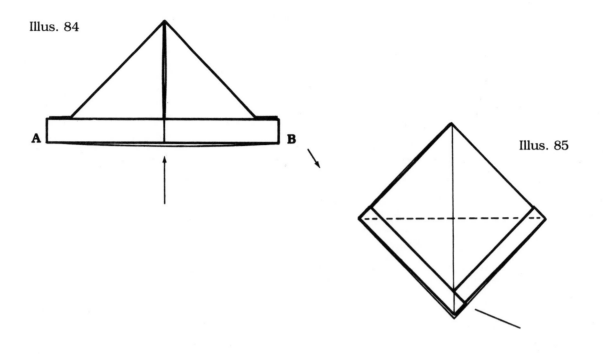

Illus. 84

A     B

Illus. 85

At this point you could stop folding and you'd have a little hat, but let's move on. Pull the sides of the project away from each other at the point shown by the arrow in Illus. 84. Keep pulling until point A comes right over on top of point B.

Now things look pretty much like Illus. 85. The arrow in the drawing points to where one corner of paper overlaps the other. In the last step, when you opened *Gabby* and pulled until one end touched the other, you probably ended up with these little paper corners sticking straight up into the air. Just slip one corner under the other and your *Gabby* will look like the one in the drawing. Then turn it over and do the same on the other side.

The dotted line in Illus. 85 shows you the next fold. But wait. Fold only the top layer of paper up along the dotted line.

When the top layer is folded up and creased into place, your project will look like Illus. 86.

Turn the paper over and fold the other layer of paper up just as you did the first. Be careful not to let any of the paper's edges or corners slip around or get wrinkled as you do this folding.

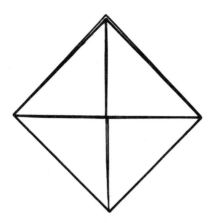

Illus. 86

*Gabby* is now seen in Illus. 87. The arrow shows where you're going to pull open the two sides of the folded paper. Pull until point C comes right over on top of point D. (We did this once before!)

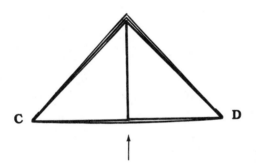

C          D

Illus. 87

By now *Gabby* is getting pretty small; it looks like Illus. 88.

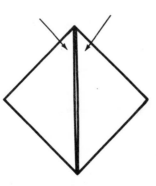

Illus. 88

Check the two arrows in Illus. 88. They indicate the two points of paper folded over the middle section. Take hold of these two paper points between your thumb and the first finger of each hand. Then slowly, carefully, pull your hands away from each other.

As the two points of paper separate, the folded paper will open up to form the small boat shown in Illus. 89. If you happen to need a little boat, stop *now*—you have one.

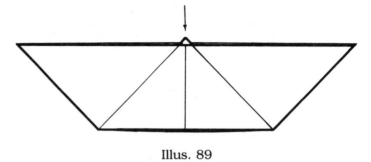

Illus. 89

Since we're making a critter and *not* a boat it's best we move on and finish *Gabby*. An arrow in Illus. 89 points to the little sail which you are going to tuck under the layer of paper at the side of the boat. Once that little pointed sail is tucked away, *Gabby* should look like Illus. 90.

The two arrows in the drawing show where to take hold of *Gabby* with your thumb and one finger. Squeeze your thumb and finger together and the *bow* and the *stern* (that's the front and the rear if you don't know boat talk) of the little boat begin to come together. You will probably have to help things along with your other hand so that the ends of the boat become the points of *Gabby's* beak.

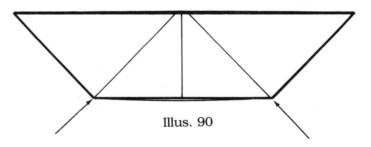

Illus. 90

Once you have the corners of the beak tucked in, *Gabby* looks just like Illus. 91. As you squeeze your thumb and finger together and then release them a bit, *Gabby's* beak opens and closes sharply.

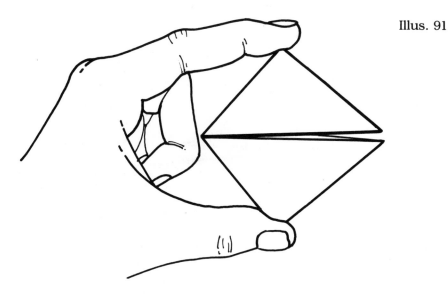

Give *Gabby* some eyes (shown in Illus. 92). If you wish, add some teeth to put a little "bite" into *Gabby's* nips.

*Gabby* is quite strong and can pick up a surprising number of objects. It can also nip people's ears and the backs of their hands as well. You should be careful who and how hard your *Gabby* nips or you may get yourself and *Gabby* into hot water.

Oh no! Eaten by my own creation!

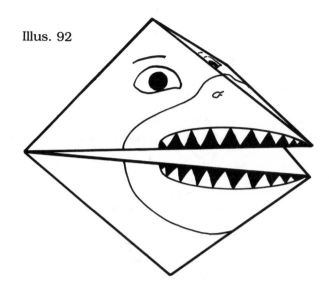

Illus. 92

Make other *Gabby* models larger or smaller than this one. Now that you see how the folding is done, it takes only a minute to make a new one.

Don't turn against me, I'm your friend!

# · 3 ·
# The Sky's the Limit

# THE SKY'S THE LIMIT

Just about everyone has built towers, houses, and other buildings using building blocks. Walls, pyramids, and other structures appear almost magically as you stack one block on top of another.

Here's your chance to go into the "construction business" in a big way. It's also a great way to use the sides of empty cereal boxes and other such containers.

In this chapter you'll discover how to put together modern buildings and futuristic structures—the things you never dreamed of building with your building blocks. You'll be using these building pieces over and over. It's a good idea to have a box (such as an empty cereal box) in which to keep each set of building pieces.

The great thing about each of the building pieces you'll be making is you don't have to make an entire set at once. Make a few pieces of each size and do some building. See which pieces and which sizes you use most often. The next time you want to go into the "building business," make a few more pieces of the most useful size. You can paint the plain side of your construction pieces, or you could use them the way they are. This is entirely up to you.

Now let's see how to make these construction sets. You just might become a master builder.

## Panel Construction

Empty cereal boxes or other cardboard boxes are perfect for making construction panels. Old manila file folders work well, too.

Panel construction pieces are easy to make and give you a terrific variety of building possibilities. Although they're easy to make, don't rush and become careless. Each piece needs to be measured and cut exactly in order to have your finished structures with even sides and no bends in the building panels.

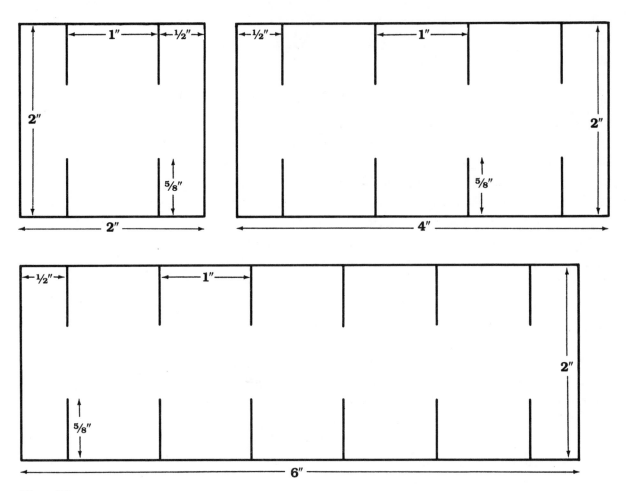

Illus. 93

To get into the panel construction business, let's begin by measuring and cutting one each of the three pieces shown in Illus. 93. These three types of panels will give you enough variety to start building almost at once.

Study Illus. 93 carefully. Check the height of all three panels. They are each exactly two inches high. Notice that the distance between the slits is exactly one inch. Check the distance between the first and last cuts and each end of the panel. This space is one-half inch. If you wish to make the end section three-fourths an inch wide, fine. Just make the ends of *every panel* the same width so your buildings look even and straight.

Finally, check the depth of the slits. They are all five-eighths inch deep. They really only need to be one-half inch deep—the panels are just two inches high. The extra one-eighth inch gives you just enough leeway so that no panel will ever stick up higher than it should.

Let's go to work. Measure carefully and make one piece of each size shown in Illus. 93. Be sure the bottom cuts or slots are exactly opposite those on the top of each panel. If you wish, you can make the cuts just a bit wider than one scissor-cut by very carefully cutting a tiny bit of material off each side of the slit.

The three pieces you just made are going to be your patterns for all the panels of these three sizes. These patterns are called templates. Builders use templates to lay out many pieces that are exactly the same size.

Here's how to use your templates. Cut a number of panels exactly the same size. Let's begin with the smallest of the three panels. Cut a dozen or so pieces two inches high and two inches wide. If you decide to make the ends stick out three-fourths inch, make the pieces two and one-half inches wide.

Place your template on top of each blank piece (in turn). Draw the cut lines using either a pencil or a ballpoint pen. Do all the pieces one after each other. Illus. 94 shows how to use the template.

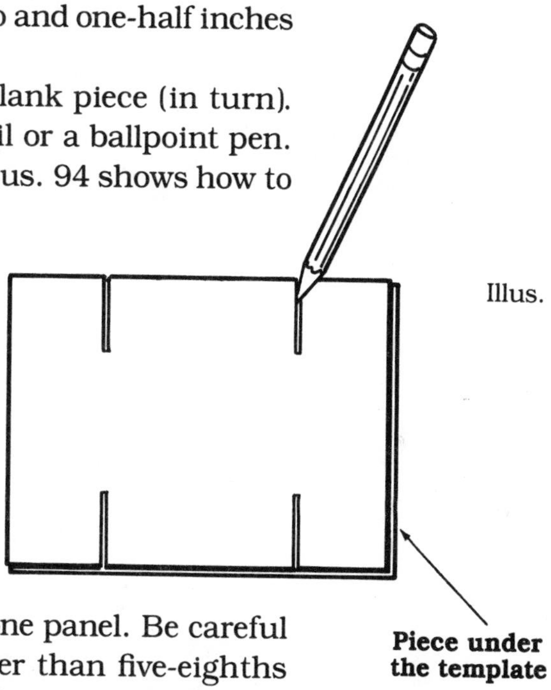

Illus. 94

**Piece under the template**

Use your scissors to cut the slits in one panel. Be careful to make the cuts straight and no longer than five-eighths inch deep. Take your time and do a perfect job. Spend a few extra minutes getting things right the first time, or you'll have to redo some pieces at a time when you'd rather be building with them.

Here's a hint. Don't try to speed things up by cutting two or three panels at once. When you attempt to hold two or three panels on top of each other they slip as you cut into the thick material. When they slip, the panels will have crooked slits. Also, when the panels slip, the slots of the bottom panels will have uneven spaces between their slots.

Cut one at a time—it's slow, but it's worth it.

Once you have made a dozen or so of the smallest panels, move on and make a dozen middle-sized panels and then a dozen of the largest ones. Now you're ready to see what sorts of structures you can build.

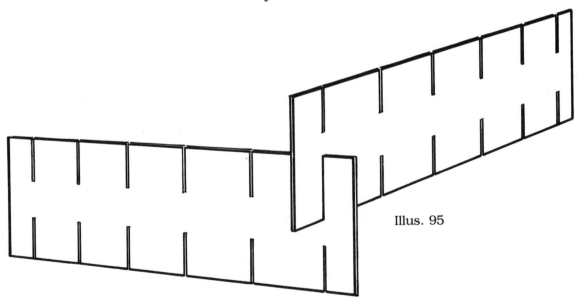

Illus. 95

Illus. 95 shows how the panels interlock to allow you to build simple or very complicated structures. Just slip one panel over another so that the two slots interlock. That's all there is to it. Try some building ideas with the panels you

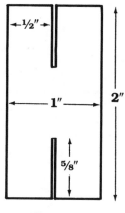

Illus. 96

made to see how the pieces fit together. Now that you have an idea of some of the possibilities, let's see what you can do to give yourself more building options.

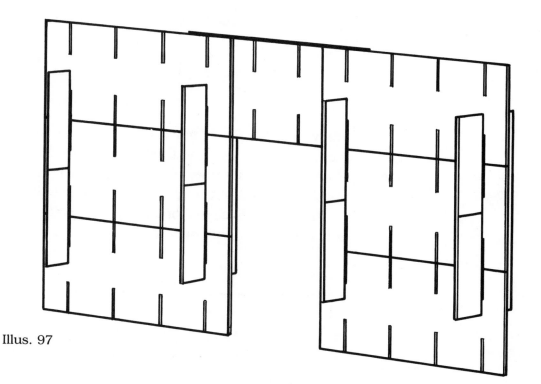

Illus. 97

Illus. 96 shows you the plan for a specialized panel. Since it is only one inch wide, it has only two slots; one in the top and one in bottom. If you decided to make your ends three-fourths inch wide, you'll always add one-fourth of an inch to each end of each panel. In this case, the panel would become one and one-half inches wide and the slot would be three-fourths inch from the side.

This little panel is used when you want to have an open window or doorway in a large wall. Illus. 97 shows you how to use these one-slot panels in this manner.

By now you have done enough building with your panels to discover that you have a space at the bottom of some of your walls and another at the top of half the walls when you finish building. Illus. 98 shows this space.

Illus. 98

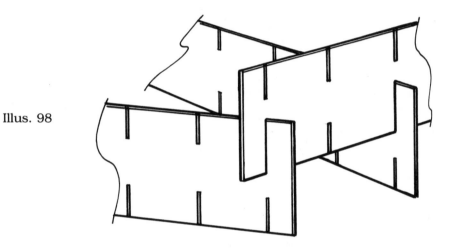

Illus. 99 shows a special sort of panel you can use to avoid having spaces at the bottoms and the tops of walls. Illus. 99 shows a panel that is only one inch high. This panel has slots cut in only one side of the panel. Use a panel such as this to fill in the space at the bottom or the space at the top of a wall; you won't have to worry about the gaps seen in Illus. 98.

Illus. 99

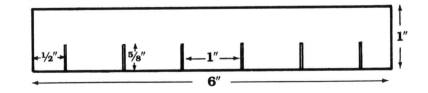

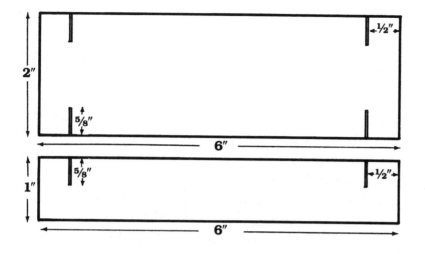

Illus. 100

Make some panels of various lengths. Panels of various lengths give you a chance to put more variety into your building program. You will find that panels eight inches long with eight slots are quite useful. Longer panels are just right for the sides of buildings.

If you want to build structures with lots of straight sides, and without lots of corners, windows, and doors, you may want to make a few panels such as the ones shown in Illus. 100.

These panels have the slots only at either end. Since they do not have the middle slots, they are quick to make. You can make these panels either two inches high with slots on the top and the bottom or one inch tall with slots only on one side. Don't make very many of these panels until you are sure you will need them.

Illus. 101 shows a construction hint you may find useful. By overlapping horizontal panels (as seen in the drawing), you can make walls just about any length you choose.

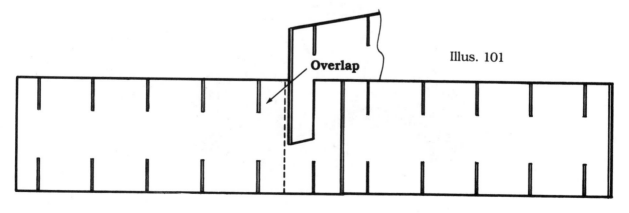

**Overlap**

Illus. 101

Use a one-slot panel or the end of a longer panel to join two horizontal panels together. The dotted line in the drawing shows how one panel overlaps behind the other panel.

Keep adding panels as you need them. Take good care of those you make, so that your set of panel-construction pieces will last for many building sessions. If a panel is damaged, throw it away; it takes only a minute to make a new one. Paint or color the panels, or use them just as they come from the cereal box.

It is all right to make panels with the slots further apart than the one inch shown. Slots spaced one and one-fourth inches or one and one-half inches apart will work perfectly. Just measure your templates carefully before you start making a stack of panels. The important thing is to space and make every slot in every panel exactly the same.

Panel construction lets you build high, wide, and handsome structures. If you find things are not going the way you want, simply slip a few panels apart and *change* your building. From there on, the sky's the limit!

How many of these do you think it would take to build the Empire State Building?

# Hollow Block Construction

Let's go on to making hollow blocks. We'll begin with a square hollow block. To make this fantastic building block, study the plan shown in Illus. 102.

Pay careful attention to the distance between the slots at the top and bottom, as well as the distance from the ends of

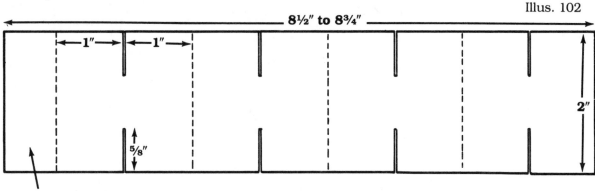

**Flap**

the material to the slots. As you study Illus. 102, look at the four dotted lines. These are exactly one inch from the slots. These dotted lines are going to be fold lines when you form your hollow block.

Carefully score cardboard with the tip of a dull table knife in order to make it fold evenly and cleanly. Place a ruler along the fold line you need to score. Hold the knife right down by the tip and press down firmly as you follow the edge of the ruler. This gives you a nice, straight crease along which to fold. Score each dotted line in order to make the folds absolutely straight so you end up with a perfectly square block.

Cut out one piece exactly like the one shown in Illus. 102. Cut the slots but don't score or fold it. Use it as your template just as you did for the panel construction pieces. Mark-

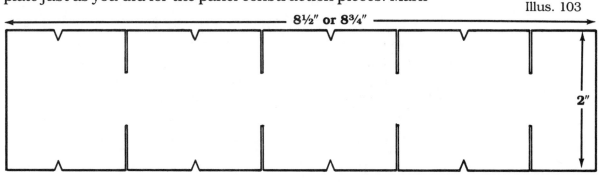

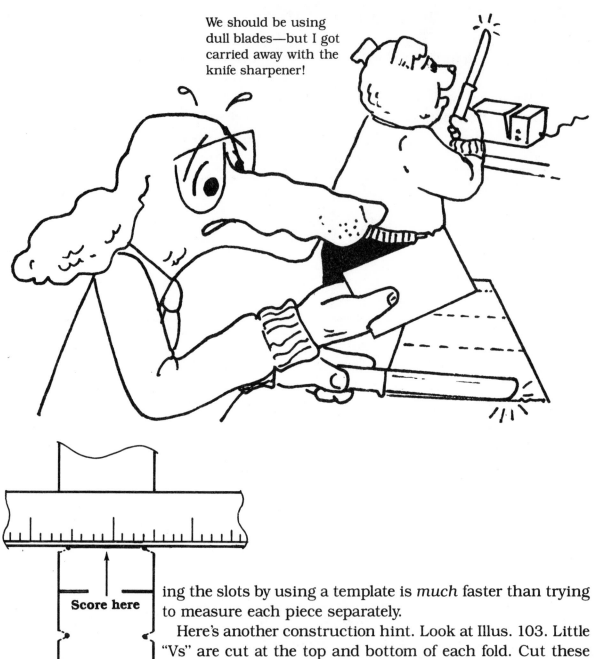

We should be using dull blades—but I got carried away with the knife sharpener!

**Score here**

Illus. 104

ing the slots by using a template is *much* faster than trying to measure each piece separately.

Here's another construction hint. Look at Illus. 103. Little "Vs" are cut at the top and bottom of each fold. Cut these little "Vs" into your template. Make certain the point in each "V" is exactly on a fold line.

When you place your template on a piece of material, use the point of your pencil or ballpoint pen to place a dot on the edge of the block material every place there is a "V." All you'll need to do to score the fold is to place your ruler beside the "Vs" and score along the edge. Illus. 104 shows the ruler lined up properly.

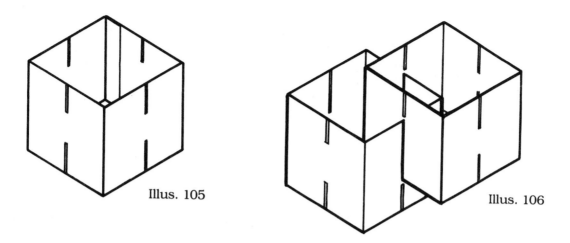

Illus. 105

Illus. 106

Cut the slots a bit wider than one scissor cut (just as you probably did for the panel construction pieces). Make the slots five-eighths of an inch deep. Make your first scissor cut and then snip off a tiny bit of material from one side of the cut to widen the slot.

Once a piece is slotted and scored, fold it along the four fold lines to form a hollow block. Tuck the end flap inside

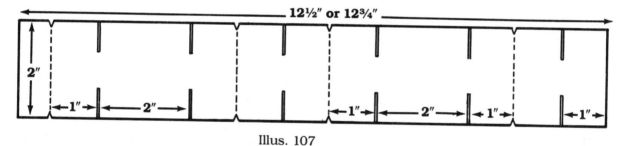

Illus. 107

and tape or glue it firmly into place. If you use tape, tape both loose ends, or your block's flap is likely to come loose. Illus. 105 shows your hollow block completed.

In Illus. 106 you see how two blocks fit together. These building blocks allow you to build all kinds of modern and futuristic structures.

For variety, you could make a hollow rectangle just as easily as a hollow square. The drawing in Illus. 107 shows how to design a two-inch by four-inch rectangular block.

Pay very close attention to the measurements on the two four-inch sides. See that there are two slots on each of the longer sides of your rectangular building block. Each of these slots is one inch from the fold—this leaves two inches

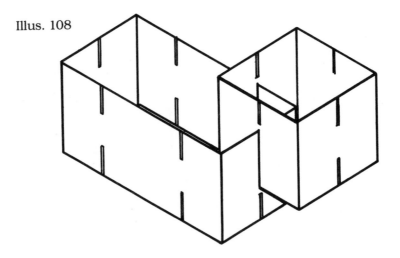

Illus. 108

between the slots on the block's long side. This is very important because the square blocks have to fit over the corners of the rectangular blocks. Illus. 108 shows how a square block fits over a rectangular block.

Don't make too many of the rectangular building blocks until you see how you like them—you may discover you prefer the square hollow blocks.

Paint or crayons give these blocks color, but there is nothing wrong with using the material just as it comes from cereal boxes or other boxes. If you turn the advertising side out, your hollow blocks will have some color to begin with.

The terrific thing about these blocks is that you can use them with your panel construction set. They should interlock perfectly. Combine the two sets of construction forms— you'll have many more opportunities for constructing interesting buildings.

Illus. 109

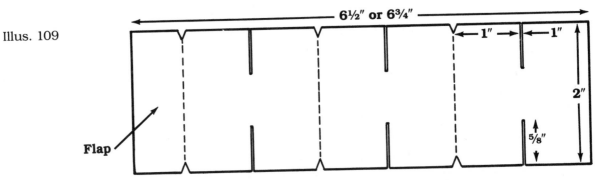

To add still *more* variety make a triangular hollow building block. Illus. 109 shows the template plan for this block.

Be sure to notice there are just three sides, rather than four. Also note the little "Vs" which are cut at the ends of the folds on the template. You can use this template just like the other templates.

Locate the slots exactly one inch from each fold. Cut them five-eighths of an inch deep and these triangular blocks may be used alone or will interlock with the blocks and panels you've already made.

Be sure to tape or glue the flap securely into place and remember to widen the slots so that they're a bit wider than just one scissor cut.

Make a dozen or so triangular hollow blocks and see how you like them. Experiment with ways to use them with the flat panels and other blocks. Make more as you need them.

You made some panels which were only one inch high and had slots cut in just one side—you used them to fill in spaces at the tops and bottoms of structures. You can also make a few special square, rectangular, or triangular blocks which are only one inch high. Illus. 110 shows the plan for making one of the short square blocks.

Illus. 110

**Flap**

This is a closet, not a lumber yard! Straighten this up!

Cut, score, and fold these half-sized hollow blocks just as you did the others. They will come in handy when you want to have a base or top come out even.

Have boxes or bags in which to store your building blocks. Parents and other family members sometimes get a bit upset if you leave your materials scattered all over the floor or just piled in a corner.

## Log Construction

You've probably seen sets of wooden building-logs. You might even own a set or you have at least played with these building-logs. Now you'll discover how to make a set of paper logs which will work the same way. You'll construct triangular logs, rather than round or square logs. There's a good reason for this. Since you'll be building hollow logs, stick to triangular ones—they'll hold their shape. Square paper logs fold up and flatten out—that takes all the fun out of building with them. Round logs need so many layers of paper it becomes almost impossible to cut notches in them.

For your first log, use paper instead of cardboard—paper's easier to cut and fold than cardboard. Besides, paper logs are solid enough for most building needs.

Notebook paper or typing paper will both work, but you should use slightly stiffer paper. Use what you have, but don't use cereal-box cardboard until you see how well paper works.

Begin by making a building log with two notches in it, one at either end. The plan for this log is shown in Illus. 111.

Pay careful attention to the measurements on the plan. You'll use most of these same measurements for logs of other lengths.

It is extremely important that you follow these measurements *exactly* when you construct your triangular logs. Otherwise the logs won't interlock properly.

The three dotted lines in Illus. 111 are fold lines. Since you are using paper for your first log, you'll find that the pressure of your pencil or ballpoint pen point will make it easy to fold along these lines. Just draw the fold line on the paper along the edge of a ruler and the paper will almost fold itself.

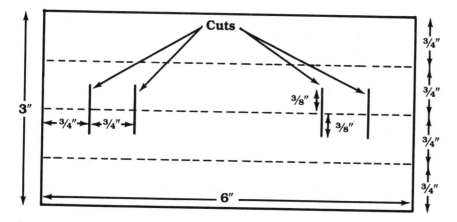

Cuts

3"

3/4" 3/4"

3/8"

3/8"

6"

3/4"

3/4"

3/4"

3/4"

If you use cardboard, score these lines before folding the logs into shape.

Study the cut lines. Each of these cut lines is exactly half the distance between the fold lines. This makes them three-eighths inch from the fold to the middle of the adjoining sides of the logs. The cuts are exactly three-fourths inch from end to end.

Illus. 112 shows an easy way to make these cuts. See how the log is folded along the middle fold line. Now all you can see is one cut line which is three-eighths inch long. Cut it while the material is folded.

Do the same for the other cut lines and unfold the paper partway. Stop unfolding when the bottom edges are about an inch apart.

Now comes the tricky part. While you hold the log partly unfolded with one hand, use the other to push down on the fold line between the two cuts. The arrow shown in Illus. 113 shows you where to push.

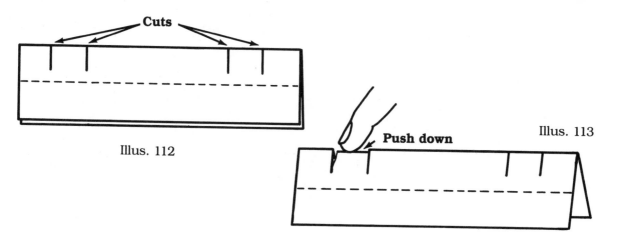

Cuts

Push down

Illus. 113

Illus. 112

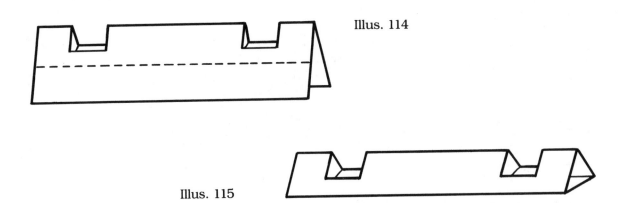

Illus. 114

Illus. 115

What you want to accomplish is to turn the material between the cuts inside out so that the fold line ends up down and inside the log. Once the material between the cuts turns inside out, you have formed the notch at one end of the log. Now do the same for the other notch. Your first log now looks like the one shown in Illus. 114.

Form the log by folding it along the three fold lines to make a triangular log. One side should overlap another.

Glue or tape the overlapping side firmly into place and your finished log looks just like the one shown in Illus. 115.

Glue works better than tape does, since it holds the overlapping flap for the entire length of the log. If you do use tape, use three or four short pieces and space them evenly along the length of the log. Make sure to tape both ends and then a couple of spots in between.

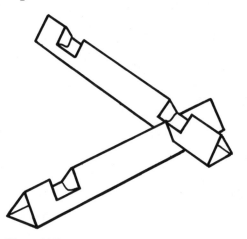

Illus. 116

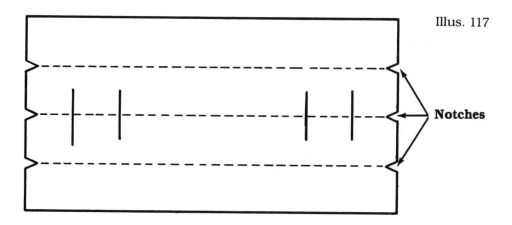

**Notches**

Make a few logs to get the feel of it. Fit their ends together as shown in Illus. 116.

Make a template so you can build a number of logs without having to stop and measure each one. You know how helpful a template is from your previous construction work.

Remember how you cut a little notch at the end of each slot for the panel template? This time cut that notch for each end of the fold in your log's template. Illus. 117 shows these notches in place on the template.

Just make a dot at the point of each notch on the log material. While the template is still in place, draw the cut lines on the log so that when you lift the template these cuts will be in their proper places.

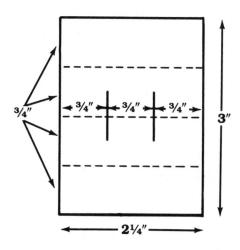

Illus. 118

Calm down, friend!
Rome wasn't built in
a day.

When you lift the template, use a ruler to draw a firm line between each pair of dots and you're ready to fold.

After you connect the dots for the folds, fold the logs in the middle and make the cuts. Glue or tape the log and it's ready to use.

It takes a bit of time to construct enough logs to begin building. Just remember—Rome wasn't built in a day. You won't make all the logs you want in one session. You're better off making a few logs each time you get ready to build.

Illus. 118 shows the plan for making a log with just one notch. Logs of this sort are used to hold longer logs together for doors, windows, and other openings.

Illus. 119 gives you the measurements for a long log with three notches. If you want to make bigger and longer logs, Illus. 120 shows the measurements for one with four notches in it.

If you decide to make logs stronger than those made from typing paper or stiff notebook paper, try making some of the short logs using file card material. Use a ballpoint pen to score the folds easily on such material.

Manila folders also make good log-building material. Depending upon the weight of the folder you may be able to

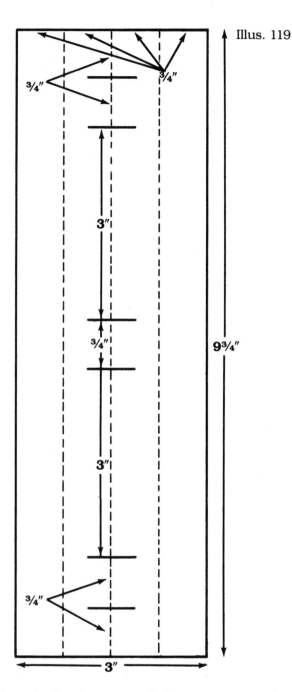

Illus. 119

9¾"

3"

3"

¾"

3"

¾"

¾"

¾"

3"

score the folds with a ballpoint pen. Otherwise, use the point of a dull table knife.

If you use cereal-box material, score the folds with a dull table knife. Lay the ruler on the material so it connects the two dots you marked when you used the template. While holding the ruler firmly in place, score the fold using the table knife. This will save you the bother of drawing the fold and then scoring it.

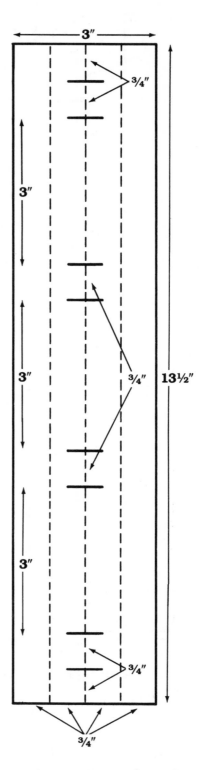

Take your time when making these fantastic construction logs. Each log must be cut and folded exactly right or it will be twisted, or off center, or just unfit for building.

# · 4 ·
# Hop, Flip, and Move

# HOP, FLIP, AND MOVE

All it takes is a bit of cutting and folding to make the paper toys in this chapter. Once the cuts are made and the folds are in place, all of these toys have one thing in common. They all move. Some hop. Others flip. One pecks at the table top and some have moving mouths and beaks.

These *Hop, Flip, and Move* toys are fun to play with and are terrific when it comes to entertaining others.

## Champion Jumping Frog

It takes just a few easy folds to turn a file card into a *Champion Jumping Frog*. This frog probably won't win any frog-jumping contests but it's still a champion. Fold it and see for yourself.

A four-by-six-inch file card is perfect for your first *Champion Jumping Frog*. A smaller file card will work perfectly, however, as will a piece of file folder.

Begin by folding the corner over, and along the dotted line as shown in Illus. 121. Crease the fold well and then unfold the card.

Illus. 122 shows the first fold in place. Your next fold will be along the dotted line. Once again, make this fold, crease it, then unfold the card.

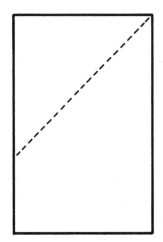

Illus. 121                              Illus. 122

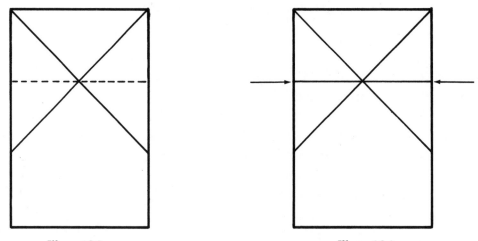

Illus. 123

Illus. 124

The next fold is shown by the dotted line in Illus. 123. This fold must come right through the point at which the two creases cross each other. This fold must also be made so the top of the card folds away from you. It's probably easier to make this fold if you turn the card over and fold the top down.

Crease the fold and turn the card back over. At this point the two diagonal folds have formed little valleys and the fold you just made sticks up towards you like a tiny mountain.

Push in at both sides of the card where the arrows are in Illus. 124. This will cause the sides to come together and the top to fold down. Your card should look just like the one shown in Illus. 125.

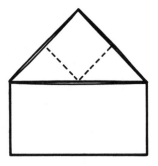

Illus. 125

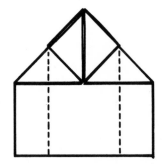

Illus. 126

Illus. 127

The two dotted lines in Illus. 125 show you where to make your next pair of folds. Fold up the top layer of card, which is really two layers thick.

When both corners are folded up, they'll meet at the top of the card as shown in Illus. 126. The two dotted lines in Illus. 126 will be your next folds. With these two folds made, the card should look like Illus. 127.

Now fold up the bottom of the card along the dotted line shown in Illus. 127. Bring the bottom of the card up so it almost reaches the point (as shown in Illus. 128).

Now fold along the dotted line shown in Illus. 129. Bring the top of the card down on the dotted line so it almost reaches the bottom. Illus. 130 shows the completed final fold.

Turn your *Champion Jumping Frog* over. The two folded points drop down to form the frog's front legs, shown in Illus. 131.

Illus. 128

Illus. 129

Illus. 130

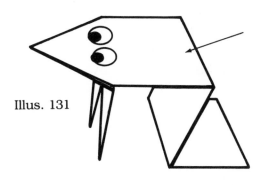

Illus. 131

Push down on the rear of the frog at the point shown by the arrow in the drawing. Let the tip of your finger slide off the frog's tail. This lets the fold spring up and causes the frog to jump. Your frog will probably want to do a flip when it jumps. Experiment to see how far you have to push it down to get it to do a complete flip in midair and land on its feet—it will usually land on its head. If you want, draw or color a pair of huge eyes to give your *Champion Jumping Frog* a bit of character.

Experiment a bit with new frogs by changing the locations of the folds in Illus. 127 and Illus. 129. By giving a frog longer legs and less body you can change the way it jumps. You might try to make another frog out of a smaller piece of material.

*Champion Jumping Frogs* are terrific toys for rainy days or when you have small children to entertain.

# A Stand-Up Sort of Guy

Here's a terrific paper toy—it's also a *traditional* paper toy. The *Stand-Up Sort of Guy* has been around for hundreds of years. No one has any idea who first learned how to fold this toy. Now that you have that bit of information in mind, let's see how to make your *Stand-Up Sort of Guy*.

Begin with a square piece of paper. Notebook paper or typing paper will work just fine. Since you folded the paper on the diagonal in order to make it square you already have the middle fold shown in Illus. 132.

If you happen to have a supply of square, unfolded paper around, then just fold one corner over to the opposite corner so that your paper has the middle crease in it.

Now make the two folds called for as shown by the pair of dotted lines in Illus. 132. Make sure you fold over each edge so the edges come right to the middle fold.

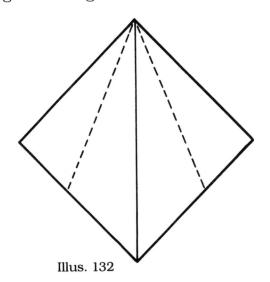

Illus. 132

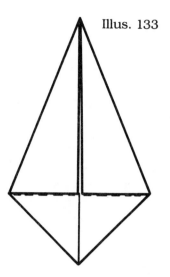

Illus. 133

Once these folds are in place, the *Stand-Up Guy* is shown in Illus. 133. The dotted line shown in the drawing tells where you'll be making your next fold. Fold the bottom point

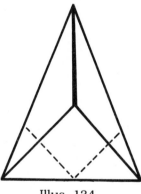

Illus. 134

up along the dotted line. This brings your project to Illus. 134.

Now fold the two corners in towards the middle fold, but don't bring the edges of the paper quite to the fold this time. Make your folds so that the edges of the paper stop just short of reaching the middle fold. Try to leave about a one-eighth-inch space between the two folded edges. Check Illus. 135 to see this space before you make the two folds.

It's again time to fold the bottom point of paper up. Illus. 135 shows this fold.

Once you've made that fold, things should look like Illus. 136. There are two dotted lines indicating another pair of folds to be made. No, the artist didn't make a mistake and repeat a previous illustration. You're going to fold the two corners over towards the middle fold once again.

Just as before, leave about a one-eighth-inch space between the edges of the two folded corners so that they don't *quite* meet along the center fold.

Be careful making this fold. By now you are working with several layers of paper, and it's easy to let them slip a bit, so your folds might not be as perfect as they should be.

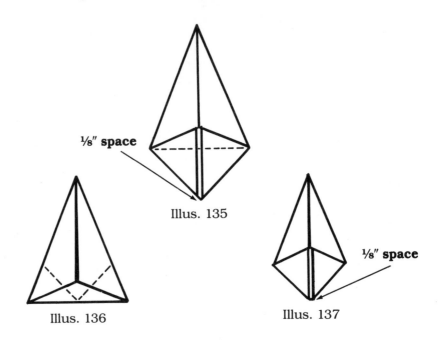

⅛″ **space**

Illus. 135

Illus. 136

⅛″ **space**

Illus. 137

With these folds in place, the *Stand-Up Sort of Guy* is shown in Illus. 137. Now fold the two sides together along the middle fold.

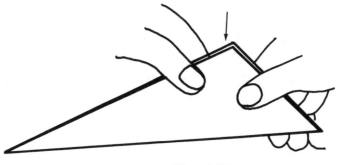

Illus. 138

When you do this, you'll probably discover that your *Guy* wants to unfold. To help keep things together, grasp the thick layer of folded paper between your thumbs and the fingers of both hands (as shown in Illus. 138) and then bend or wiggle the paper from side to side. This will help settle things inside the folded paper.

Sometimes you'll get a little tear along the middle fold at the point shown by the arrow in Illus. 138. Don't worry—this won't bother the little *Guy*.

Hold the two sides of the project together and place it on a table in the position shown in Illus. 139.

Release the *Stand-Up Guy*. Within a few seconds it should suddenly tip up so it stands upright, as seen in Illus. 140.

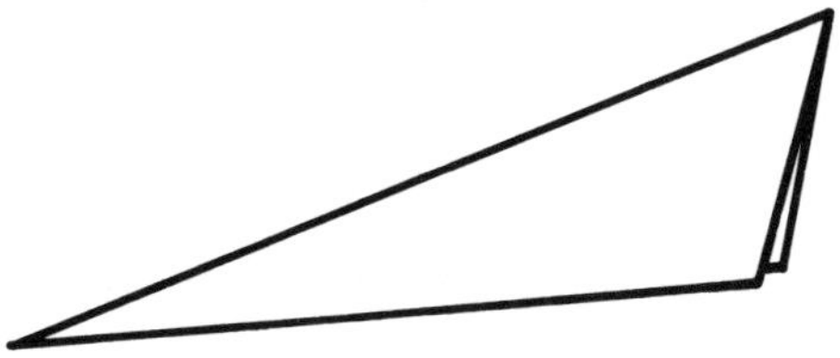

Illus. 139 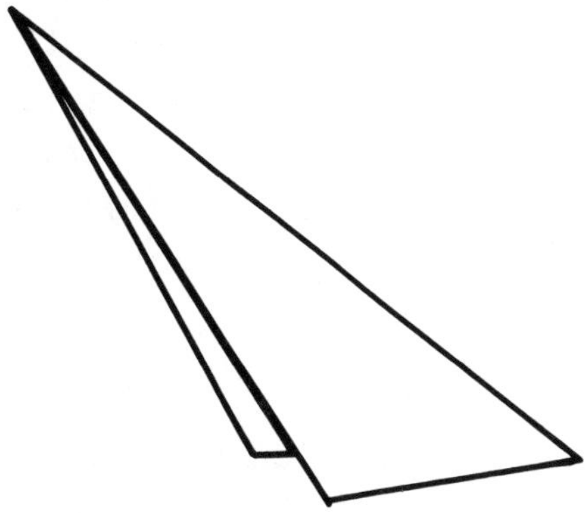                                                                 Illus. 140

It stands because the folded paper inside comes apart. This changes the toy's center of balance and causes it to stand up (or on its head, if you please). Refold the toy by pressing both sides together and it will stand up again.

If your little *Guy* won't stand up, it is because the paper inside is not moving. Try making another model and leave a bit more space when you fold the corners in towards the middle fold.

If your little *Guy* stands up instantly and you'd like to slow it down, fold your next model with the corners a bit closer to the middle fold.

This is a terrific little toy to amaze and amuse others. You set it on one side—and suddenly it's standing upright. Naturally your friends think you're a genius. Small children are entertained and delighted as the *Stand-Up Sort of Guy* is willing to stand up again and again.

# Flipper

This terrific action toy will give you lots of fun. If you use it at the wrong time and in the wrong place, it will also give you loads of problems, but that's entirely up to you.

You'll need an eight-inch square sheet of really stiff paper. You can make your first *Flipper* from notebook paper to see how it works but you're going to need stiff, tough paper to hold up when you start playing with *Flipper* and going for distance records.

Begin by folding the paper in the middle and creasing the fold. Unfold the paper and you're at the point shown in Illus. 141.

When you fold the paper along the two dotted lines seen in Illus. 141, make certain the edges of the paper come right to the middle fold. Crease these two folds and unfold the paper one more time.

Now your folded paper looks like the drawing shown in Illus. 142.

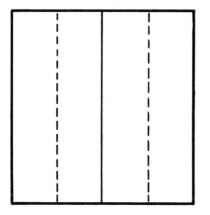

Illus. 141

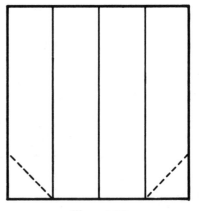

Illus. 142

Your next step is to fold both bottom corners up along the dotted lines seen in Illus. 142. Make sure the corners come right to the folds in the paper.

With this bit of folding complete, *Flipper* is seen in Illus. 143.

It's time now to fold both sides in towards the middle. Just fold them along the folds you made a moment ago. Your project now appears as seen in Illus. 144.

The dotted line shown in Illus. 144 shows where you'll make your next fold. Make this fold just a little less than one inch from the top of the paper.

Once you've finished this fold, *Flipper* looks like the drawing shown in Illus. 145.

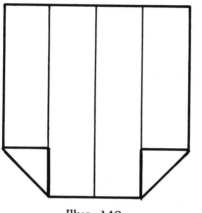

Illus. 143

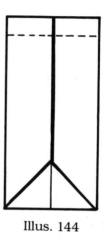

Illus. 144

Turn the paper over so that it looks like Illus. 146. Fold the bottom corner over to the opposite side along the dotted line so that *Flipper* looks like Illus. 147.

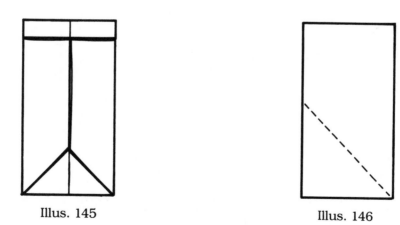

Illus. 145

Illus. 146

Unfold the paper and you've reached Illus. 148. Your next fold is along the dotted line in the drawing.

With that fold in place you're at Illus. 149. Once again unfold the paper and you're now at Illus. 150.

Fold the bottom of the paper under along the dotted line seen in Illus. 150.

Crease the fold well and turn the paper over. You've reached the stage seen in Illus. 151.

Illus. 147

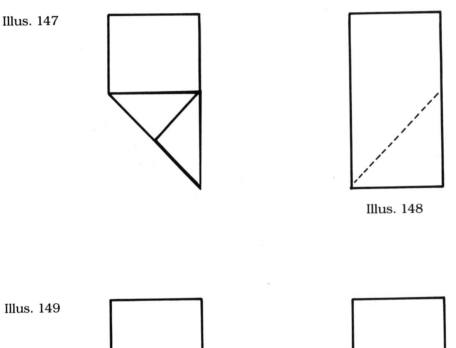

Illus. 148

Illus. 149

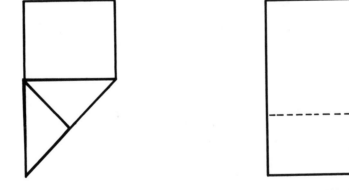

Illus. 150

Take hold of the paper in both hands at the points indicated by the two arrows in Illus. 151.

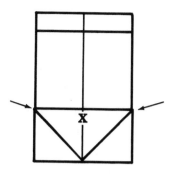

Illus. 151

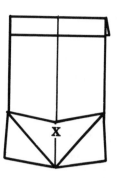

Illus. 152

Push your hands together just a bit and the part of *Flipper* marked with an "X" will push out towards you so it looks like Illus. 152.

It's now time to do a tricky fold which gets *Flipper* ready for action. Illus. 153 shows two dotted lines at the top of the paper. You need to fold only the top layer of paper (the flap) up along these dotted lines. Don't fold yet!

Don't tear the paper while making these folds. Take your time. Work with one side at a time and let *Flipper* fold up along its middle fold as you press the new fold into place.

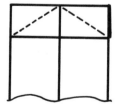

Illus. 153

Pocket for paper wad

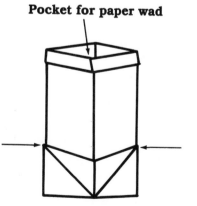

Illus. 154

Use the thumbs and fingers of both hands to coax the folds into the top layer.

Second, as you begin to crease these two little folds into place, the two tabs of paper under the section you are folding will begin to overlap. Now your *Flipper* looks like the one in Illus. 154.

Tear off a piece of scrap paper about two inches square and wad it into a little ball. Drop that paper wad into the little pocket that you just formed at the top of the project. The arrow at the top of the drawing shows this pocket.

Turn *Flipper* around so all the folds and points are facing away from you. Hold both sides of your *Flipper* at the points indicated by the large arrows in Illus. 154. Be sure you are holding both the front and back layers.

Push your hands together just a bit. Now, separate your hands with a quick, sharp jerk. Don't jerk hard enough to tear *Flipper*!

The paper wad will be flipped out of its pocket and into the air. With just a couple of practice flips you should be able to propel the paper wad anywhere from six to ten feet. Whether you can hit a specific target is another question.

*Flipper* needs to be made of pretty stiff, tough paper. It's easy to tear notebook paper when you give *Flipper* that quick, sudden jerk.

If you're into experimenting, make another *Flipper* out of a rectangle of paper. It may give you more range when you flip the paper wad into space. Also, try a slightly larger paper wad and see whether this improves distance or accuracy.

# Beaky

*Beaky's* name will make perfect sense once the project is finished. Begin by turning a piece of notebook paper or typing paper into a square sheet. When you do this you'll end up with the diagonal fold shown in Illus. 155. If you had square paper to begin with, make the diagonal fold right now.

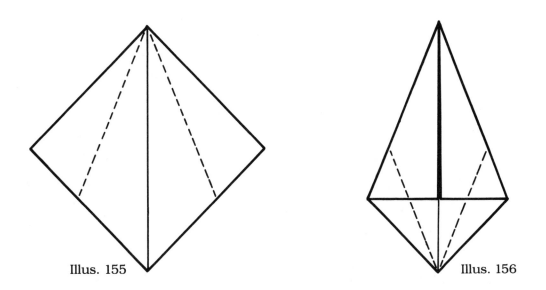

Illus. 155          Illus. 156

When you fold the two sides along the dotted lines shown in Illus. 155, be sure both sides of the paper come right to the middle fold.

Once those two folds are finished, your paper should look like the drawing shown in Illus. 156.

Your next folding step: Fold both sides of *Beaky* along the pair of dotted lines shown in Illus. 156. Be careful making these folds and the ones to come. Try to make nice, sharp creases and avoid getting wrinkles in the paper. You'll understand the warning about wrinkles just a couple of folds from now. You're now at the point shown in Illus. 157.

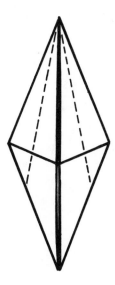

Illus. 157                    Illus. 158

Illus. 159

Illus. 160

As you make the two folds along the dotted lines shown in Illus. 157, make sure both sides of the paper come right to the middle fold. Crease these folds well.

Illus. 158 gives you a view of progress to this point. Fold up the bottom point of paper along the dotted line. Here's where you really have to avoid getting wrinkles in the paper. Take care to tuck the paper into place with your fingers when you make this fold. The inside layers usually want to bunch up and make a nasty wrinkle or two. Check Illus. 159 to see how your *Beaky* should look after that last fold.

When you fold along the dotted line in Illus. 159, you are only folding the part of *Beaky* you just folded up in the last step. Glance at Illus. 160 first to see how things look after this fold is finished. Once the fold is in place crease it well.

Illus. 161

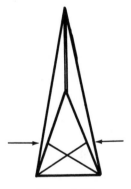

Illus. 162

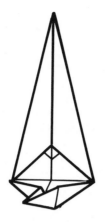

Illus. 163

Now *unfold* the fold you just made so that *Beaky* looks like Illus. 161. Make the fold along the dotted line. This fold is just the opposite of the one you just made.

Crease the fold and unfold the paper again. You're still at Illus. 161, but the dotted line in the drawing is now a fold in your project.

Check Illus. 162 for the next step—this will take just a little bit of care. Push in with your thumbs at the points shown by the two arrows. Push only on the top layer which you've been folding back and forth for the last several steps.

As you push your thumbs together, hold the main part of *Beaky* with your fingers. All you want to move and fold is the many-times-folded top layer.

As your thumbs come together, a point of paper will begin to stand up; it will also move backwards. Move your thumbs with it. You'll end up with both sides of the paper coming together and forming the point shown in Illus. 163.

Turn *Beaky* over and hold it by this point of paper. Let your thumb and forefinger rest against the little triangles which are shown by the arrows in Illus. 164.

When you squeeze your thumb and finger together, *Beaky* will begin to rise and fall. Practise just a few seconds to get the hang of this. Don't squeeze too hard. If *Beaky* doesn't want to rise and fall, make sure the middle fold forms a little mountain for its entire length.

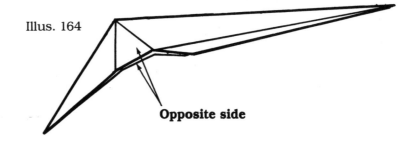

Illus. 164

**Opposite side**

Add some eyes and nostrils to the paper so it looks something like Illus. 165. You should now see why this terrific little paper toy is called *Beaky*.

Use *Beaky* as a talking puppet head, as a pointer, or to entertain others. It's fantastic fun. If you're into puppets, make two *Beaky* models and use one in either hand—they'll talk to each other.

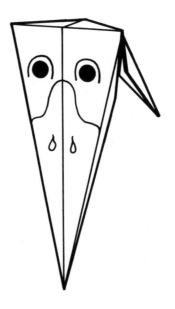

Illus. 165

# · 5 ·
# Brighten Up Your Room—Or Any Room

# BRIGHTEN UP YOUR ROOM— OR ANY ROOM

During the dull, dark days of winter, or when the rain comes pouring down, one of the best things you can do to raise your spirits is to brighten up your room.

In this chapter you'll learn to make some terrific paper room-brighteners. We'll begin with a *Whirly Twirly* and then go on to fancy paper chains—they don't need any taping or pasting to hold them together. Then we'll make some colorful paper flowers—they'll never wilt and they'll never need fresh water.

If you're preparing for a party or just *thinking* about having a party, this is the chapter for you! These room-brighteners are perfect for party decorations. They make terrific holiday decorations, as well.

## Whirly Twirly

The *Whirly Twirly* is easy to make and terrific to have as a room-brightener. This great decoration just keeps hanging around having fun.

Make your first *Whirly Twirly* using stiff paper, file cards, a piece of file folder, or cereal-box cardboard. Begin by cutting two squares of material. Each piece of square material should measure four inches on all sides.

Illus. 166 shows the first piece of material. The cut needs to be right down the middle of the square and it should be two and one-eighth inches long. The reason for that extra one-eighth inch—when you assemble the *Whirly Twirly* you won't end up with one side sticking up higher than the other. It doesn't matter if one side *does* stick up a fraction on an inch, but let's try to be perfect.

Once you've made the cut it's time to fold the piece along the two dotted lines. The left hand side is towards you. Fold the right hand side down and away from you.

If you're working with cereal-box material, it's a good idea to use a ruler and the point of a dull table knife to score the

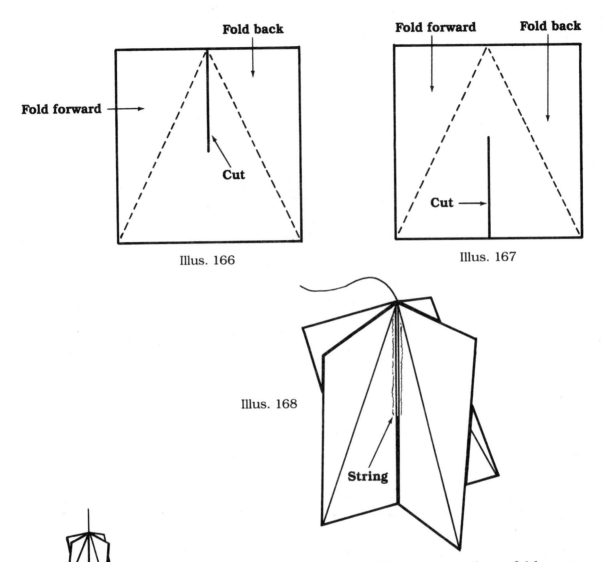

**Fold back**

**Fold forward**

**Cut**

Illus. 166

**Fold forward**     **Fold back**

**Cut** →

Illus. 167

Illus. 168

**String**

Illus. 169

folds before making them. If you score these folds, remember to score the right-hand fold on the *back* side of the material, since that fold is made down and away from you.

Now that the first piece is cut and folded, set it aside and we'll deal with the second part of the *Whirly Twirly*. This piece is shown in Illus. 167.

As you can see, the only difference in the two pieces is that the two and one-eighth-inch cut in this piece is made starting from the *bottom* of the material instead of from the top.

The folds are just the same. Again, the left hand side is folded towards you. The right-hand side is folded down and away.

When the two pieces are both cut and folded, slip them together by sliding one cut over the other cut. Try to position the two pieces so that they are at right angles to each other. Don't worry if they slip a bit, we'll take care of that right now.

Since your *Whirly Twirly* needs to hang in order to do its thing, it's time to attach a piece of string or heavy thread as a hanger. Illus. 168 shows the end of the string in its proper location.

Lay two inches (or so) of one end of the string into the corner formed where the two pieces meet. Squirt a little line of glue along the string and make sure the two pieces are

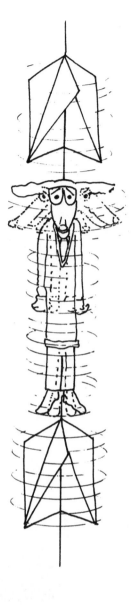

STOP! You're making both of us dizzy!

still at right angles. Use the point of a toothpick or even a pencil to push the string and the glue right into the corner.

Once the glue dries, pick up the *Whirly Twirly* by the string and blow gently on it. You'll be amazed as how easily it twirls in the air. Once a *Whirly Twirly* is hanging, it will often turn and spin when people walk by.

This terrific decoration also does a reverse spin. Once the string is tightly wound in one direction, the *Whirly Twirly* will unwind in the other direction.

Hang this toy from a curtain rod, from an overhead-lamp chain, or from a hanging-basket hook. You can also run a string from one side of the room to the other and hang one or more *Whirly Twirly* toys from that string.

Illus. 169 shows another way to use the *Whirly Twirly*. If you want to hang three or four on one string, why not begin with three-inch squares of material, or even squares a bit smaller? Another idea—make a single *Whirly Twirly* six or even eight inches square.

Now that you see how easy it is to make this room-brightener (and how great it is), you'll want to decorate some to *really* brighten up the room or the party. Do any painting or coloring *before* you cut and fold the pieces. It's lots easier that way.

Consider making the folded corners one color and the rest of each section another color. How about alternating colors so that one panel's folds match the base of the other panel? Or, maybe you'd like to have the fronts of the panels one color and the backs another. The possibilities are nearly endless.

Another great way to make your *Whirly Twirly* really terrific is to spread a thin layer of glue onto the folded-corner section. Then sprinkle glitter onto the glue. When the glue dries your *Whirly Twirly* will flash as it spins.

You can also make *Whirly Twirly* spinners using stiff colored paper. Another idea is to glue bits of foil or colored wrapping paper to your *Whirly Twirly*.

## Decorative Chains

We usually think of paper chains as Christmas or party decorations. They can also be used to help beautify any room, including yours.

The chains you'll learn to make are pretty terrific. They need neither glue nor staples to hold them together.

You can make these chains using painted or colored notebook paper, colored paper, file cards or file folders, or using cereal-box material. As with the *Whirly Twirly*, color or paint the white material before you cut the chain links.

If you wish, make your party chains using wrapping paper. Although it is often fairly lightweight, even a long chain won't tear unless someone gets really rough with it. Let's see how to make these chains.

Begin by cutting a piece of material two-inches wide and four-inches long. Fold it in the middle so it becomes a two-by-two-inch square like the one shown in Illus. 170.

Place the material in front of you so that the fold is at the bottom, as shown in the drawing.

Measure down from the top (the open side of the paper) one-half inch, and then mark that point. Measure in from each side one-half inch and then mark these points. These points should be in line with the mark you already made when you measured from the top. These marks are seen in Illus. 171.

Once you have located these points, use them to draw a line one-inch long and one-half inch from the top of the paper. This line is already drawn near the top of Illus. 172.

Measure in one-half inch from either side along the fold at the bottom. Mark these points as shown in Illus. 172.

Use a ruler and pencil to draw a straight line from each point on the fold to the corner above. This step is seen in Illus. 173.

Now mark points along the fold three-eighths inch in from the lines you just drew. These marks are seen in Illus. 174. Now connect these two marks with the one-inch-long line near the top of the material (as shown in Illus. 175) and you're ready to cut out the chain link.

Illus. 170

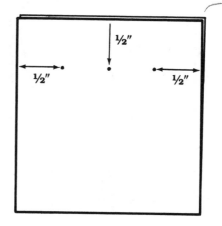

Illus. 171

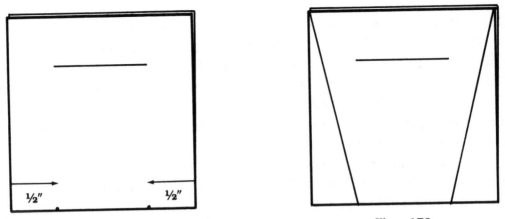

Illus. 172

Illus. 173

Cut with the material still folded. Grasp it firmly so it does not slip. If you don't you might end up with a less-than-perfect chain link.

As soon as you have cut this link, use it as a pattern for your next link. You won't have to do all this measuring for each link in your chain.

When you've cut two links, you'll see how the chain goes together. Slip one side of a link through the fold in another link (shown in Illus. 176).

Slide the link on and then turn it around. The connected links are seen in Illus. 177.

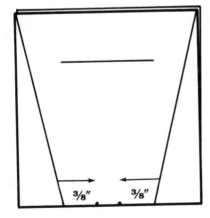

Illus. 174

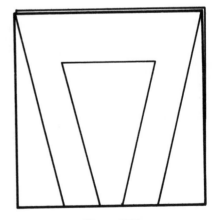

Illus. 175

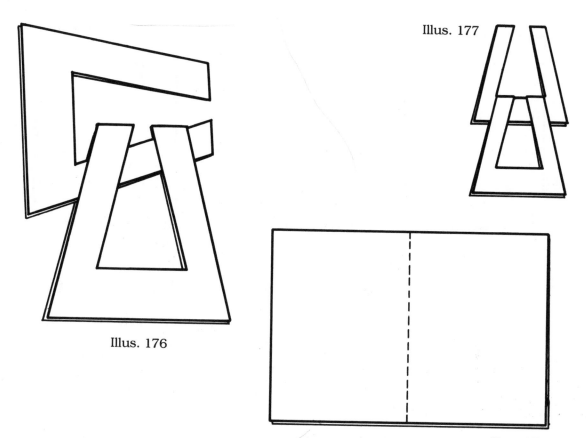

Illus. 177

Illus. 176

Illus. 178

The number of links you can join together in this manner is limitless. Your fantastic paper chain just gets longer and longer.

Before you go any further, cut a pattern or template using cereal-box material. Cut as many pieces of two-by-four-inch material as you want and then fold them double. Trace around the pattern or template to outline the chain links. After you draw a number of links, stop drawing and start cutting. If several of you are working together on this project, set up an assembly line.

Before you begin mass production, you need to make some major decisions. Do you want your chain links exactly the size you just made or would you like them larger? If you work carefully, you can make smaller links and have a delicate chain.

You can make a stronger chain if the links are wider than those you just made. You could use paper two and one-fourth inches wide or even two and one-half inches wide so you can have thicker sides for the chain links. If you're

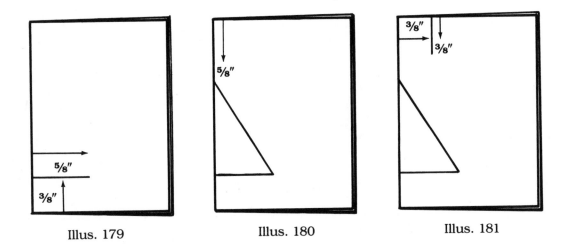

Illus. 179          Illus. 180          Illus. 181

going to paint or color the links, do that before you cut them
out.

For variety, here's another chain-link pattern you might
want to try. Begin by cutting a piece of paper three-inches
wide and four-inches high. Fold it in half along the four-inch
side so it looks like Illus. 178. The dotted line indicates your
next fold.

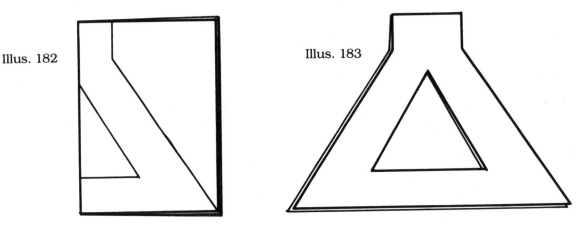

Illus. 182                    Illus. 183

After making that fold, the paper is shown in Illus. 179.
One fold is at the top and the other is at the left.

Measure up from the bottom three-eighths inch and draw
a line five-eighths inch long. This line is show in Illus. 179.

Now measure down from the top (along the left-hand fold)
and mark the point five-eighths inch from the top. Draw a
line connecting this point with the end of the first line you
drew. At this stage things should look like Illus. 180.

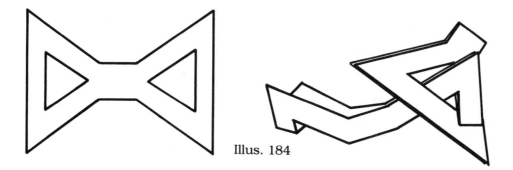

Illus. 184

Next, measure along the top fold three-eighths inch from the left-hand side and mark that point. Draw a line down from that mark three-eighths inch long. This new line appears in Illus. 181.

Finish up by connecting the end of this last line with the bottom right-hand corner and your chain-link-to-be looks like Illus. 182.

Cut out the link while the paper is still folded. Then use that link as a pattern for another link or two.

To join the links into a chain, unfold one link one fold so it looks like Illus. 183.

Unfold the second link and slip it through the middle of the first link. The two drawings in Illus. 184 show you how.

Once one link is slipped through the other, open the link you had folded along the long side, and your chain fits together like the pair of links shown in Illus. 185. Now you can make the chain as long as you wish.

Illus. 185

Using a cardboard template for a pattern, feel free to adjust the size of the links to suit yourself. After all, it's your chain.

## Pretty Posy

A posy is a flower, as you probably already know. You can make this paper flower either from colored paper or from regular notebook paper. Color the notebook paper before folding and cutting. Since this is a two-part flower, add

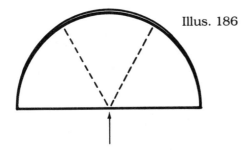

Illus. 186

Illus. 187

variety by making one part from paper of one color and the other part from paper of a different color.

Begin by cutting two circles from your paper. One circle should be about four inches across and the other should only be about three inches across. If you're drawing circles with a compass, make the sizes exact. If you use bottle lids and can bottoms as patterns, choose two about one inch different in size. Fold each circle in half so the paper looks like Illus. 186.

Your next step is to locate the middle of the circle. The arrow in Illus. 186 shows the point halfway along the folded line. If you used a compass there should be no problem. The compass hole should be the middle. If you drew around round items it's still no problem finding the halfway point along the fold. Just bring the two ends of the fold together and then pinch the middle. Don't fold it, just pinch the middle point.

Now fold each circle twice more on the dotted lines shown in Illus. 186. The half-circle is now folded into thirds. The paper should look like Illus. 187. Both folds begin at the middle point. Don't worry if your half-circles are not folded into perfect thirds. Come as close as possible.

The two dotted lines shown in Illus. 187 show you where to cut. Since you are cutting through six layers of paper, use sharp scissors and hold the paper firmly so it doesn't slip and slide as you cut. Once cutting is finished, unfold your new posy. It looks like the one shown in Illus. 188.

Each of the petals needs a fold down its middle. To do this, fold the petals in half along each of the dotted lines shown in Illus. 188.

Illus. 188

Pin

Illus. 189

Work your way around the flower, folding each opposite pair of petals to form a raised ridge through each pair. Three folds will take you all the way around—each fold takes care of two petals.

Place the smaller flower on top of the larger one, as shown in Illus. 189. Push a pin through the middles of both flower parts and mount the finished *Pretty Posy* on a corkboard or you could pin one to a curtain. The arrow in the drawing points to the pin you'll push through the flower parts.

You can color the middle of the smaller circle of petals to brighten things up. Or, cut a small circle of colored paper and push the pin through it when you pin the two larger sections together.

If you want to add variety, experiment with a three-part flower. Make the third circle smaller or larger depending upon how big you want the finished flower to be.

Other variations of *Pretty Posy* are easy to fold and cut. Begin by folding the circles in half so that they look like Illus. 190. The dotted line in the drawing shows your next, and final, fold.

Make that final fold and you've reached Illus. 191. Cut along the dotted lines in the drawing, and you'll have a flower with four petals.

Another, fancier variation, is to fold the paper double so it looks like Illus. 190. Fold again to reach Illus. 191. Now fold it in half one more time so your folded circle looks like Illus. 192. Cut along the dotted lines in the drawing—you'll have a flower with eight petals.

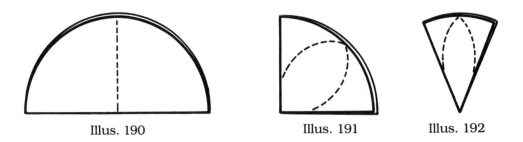

Illus. 190        Illus. 191        Illus. 192

You could make the petals a bit fancier than those in the drawing. Experiment with your scissors and create a *Pretty Posy* entirely of your own invention.

## Multifold Flower

In case you didn't know, "multi" means *many*. That should give you a clue about the number of folds it takes to create this paper flower. Don't let the name scare you away. The folds are not at all difficult to make.

Begin your *Multifold Flower* with a square piece of paper about twelve inches (or larger) on all sides. Try smaller squares of paper after you make the first one.

The *Multifold Flower* needs to be made of thin, tough paper. Thin gift-wrapping is best. Notebook paper or typing paper will both work, but not as well. Thick, colored construction paper won't work for this flower. There are too many folds to be made and construction paper will tear during the final step.

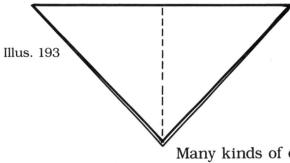

Illus. 193

Many kinds of colored gift-wrapping paper are great, as are some of the colored tissue papers used as gift wraps.

If you're using white paper and want colored flowers, you need to do the coloring before you finish folding. Make your first *Multifold Flower* without worrying about color. Once you see how it fits together—you'll know then what part of your paper needs to be colored.

Begin this terrific flower by making the diagonal fold shown in Illus. 193. The dotted line indicates your next fold.

Fold one corner of the paper over to the other along the dotted line shown in Illus. 193 and then crease the fold. Then unfold the paper so it looks like the sheet seen in Illus. 194.

The middle of the paper is where the two diagonal folds cross each other in Illus. 194. Folding the diagonal folds helped locate the center, by the way.

There are four dotted lines shown in Illus. 195. Each dotted line represents a fold you need to make. Just fold the corner of the paper over so that the point reaches the middle of the paper. Now crease the fold, and do this for all four corners.

Illus. 196 shows your paper with all four folds creased into place.

Illus. 196 also has four more dotted lines. Just as you did before, fold each corner over so that each point comes right to the middle of the paper.

When these four folds are in place and creased well, your project should look like Illus. 197.

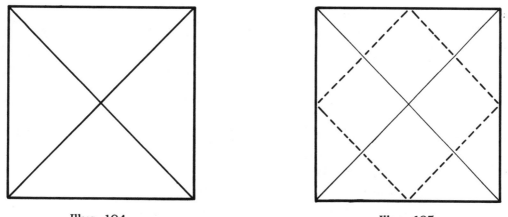

Illus. 194                              Illus. 195

There are four more dotted lines in Illus. 197. These lines indicate four more folds. Fold all four corners to the middle and crease the folds carefully. That brings us to Illus. 198. There aren't any dotted lines in Illus. 198—you're going to turn the paper over now.

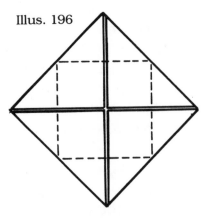

Illus. 196

In Illus. 199 you see what the paper looks like when you turn it over. There are four more dotted lines. Be of good cheer. These are your final folds.

Get a firm grip on the paper as you make these last four folds. By now your *Multifold Flower* is many layers of paper thick and it will be difficult to make these last folds without having the paper wrinkle. Take your time and make each fold so that the corners of the paper come right to the middle. Illus. 200 shows the thick packet of folded paper as it appears after these last folds.

Illus. 197

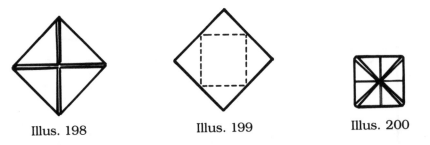

Illus. 198

Illus. 199

Illus. 200

Now comes the final step. It's the only really tricky thing about making this flower. Don't rush! Take your time, or you'll tear the paper.

Each corner of the folded paper will become a flower petal standing up from the base of the flower. In order to make these petals, you're going to turn each corner inside out. Here's how.

Illus. 201 shows one corner we're going to work with. Pick up the folded flower and press the thumb of one hand onto the point shown by the single arrow in Illus. 201. You'll push in on the two sections of folded paper in just a second.

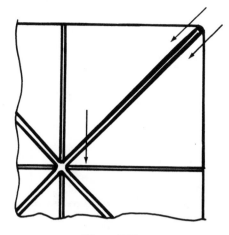

Illus. 201

Press the ball of your other thumb against the point of paper indicated by the two arrows. This thumb presses *in* and *down* when you're ready to open the petal.

On the back side of the paper a triangular fold of paper is exactly opposite the area you are pressing with your thumbs. Hook your index finger under the triangular point of paper and begin to lift it up.

Here's where you are. Your thumbs are pushing in and your index finger is lifting the fold on the opposite side of the paper. What you have to do is to turn this corner of thickly folded paper inside out. When you do, the point shown by the two arrows in the drawing will become the *inside* of the petal. The paper you lift with your index finger becomes an open petal. This petal will stand straight up.

Check Illus. 202 to see how the petal looks once you have it turned inside out and in place.

Take your time. You'll feel the paper resist you, but don't worry. Just keep up the pressure, but do it slowly. You don't want to tear the paper. This is why you're using thin, tough paper. Use your thumb to squash the point of paper you're pushing so that it is almost flat inside the petal, or you can let if form a little wad to give the inside of the petal a raised look. It's up to you.

If you get a tiny tear at the edge of a petal, your *Multifold Flower* is not ruined. Just work slowly and firmly, and you'll soon get the first petal open. After that it's easy!

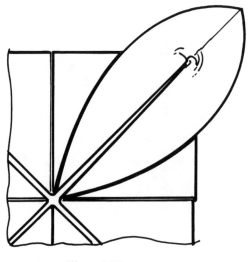

Illus. 202

Open all four petals. Decide whether you want to pin your flower somewhere or set it on a desk or table. Now that you can make this flower, you can decide whether to make other flowers of white paper and color them, or if you'll use colored paper to begin with. In spite of all the folds, this is really a terrific paper flower.

# · 6 ·
# Huff and Puff

# HUFF AND PUFF

The terrific paper toys in this chapter all require a little huffing and puffing as you play with them. You'll blow on a couple of them to make them work. Another needs only to be dropped and the air it falls through causes it to do its thing.

One toy will leave you huffing and puffing because you can't ever make it change its mind about the way it behaves.

## Spinner

Cut two four-inch squares of notebook paper and you're ready to make your first *Spinner*. Fold only one square to begin with, so just lay the second one aside for a minute or two.

Start by folding the paper in half. Illus. 203 shows how it looks with that fold in place. Fold the top down along the dotted line shown in Illus. 203. Your *Spinner* will now look like Illus. 204.

Next, fold the top layer of paper up along the dotted line shown in Illus. 204. Fold only the top layer, please!

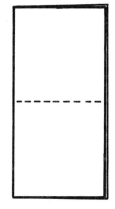

Illus. 203

Illus. 204

Illus. 205

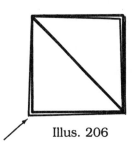

Illus. 206

As soon as you've made that fold, turn the paper over—it should look like Illus. 205.

You've got another fold coming up. The dotted line in Illus. 205 shows that fold. Once more, you'll fold only the top layer when making this fold.

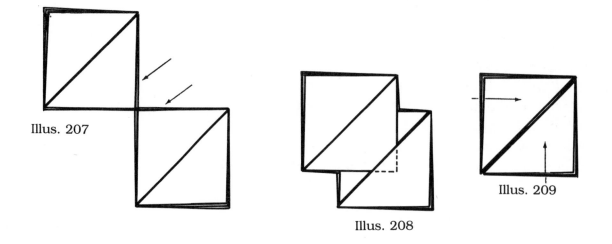

Illus. 207

Illus. 208

Illus. 209

Once this fold is made, your paper toy looks like the one shown in Illus. 206. There are two single layers of paper at the lower corner (shown by the arrow). Check your paper toy just to make certain that it's correctly folded at this point.

Lay this paper aside and fold the other square exactly as you did this one. You should end up with two sections of paper folded exactly alike.

You're really kicking up a breeze, friend!

Once both squares of paper are folded in the same way, it's time to join them together. Illus. 207 shows how to line up the two squares properly. The arrows in the drawing point to the corners of the folded paper having only two single layers of paper. You've turned one folded square around a half-turn, so the single layers of each square point towards each other.

Slip one square of paper over the other; the single sheets of paper slip into the triangular pockets of the other square. Illus. 208 shows this step partly finished. The dotted lines show where the single sheet of paper is slipping inside the fold on the other square. The same thing is happening on the other side of the squares.

Push the two squares all the way together so that they look like Illus. 209.

Lift up the two single sheets of paper indicated by the arrows so that they stick straight up. Do the same with the two single sheets on the other side.

Hold the *Spinner* between your thumb and your index finger as shown in Illus. 210. Blow on it and it will spin wildly.

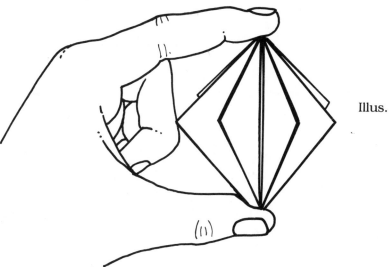

Illus. 210

Don't hold it too tightly or it won't spin. However, you have to hold it tightly enough so that the *Spinner* doesn't get blown out of your hand.

Think about coloring some of the panels one color and some another. Or, make one square from colored paper and the other from paper of a different color. When the *Spinner* is spinning rapidly, you'll have a colorful display as well. Every child in your class will want a copy of this spinning toy.

If you want to "go big time," make the squares of paper eight or so inches on each side. This large *Spinner* should be held between the index fingers of both hands.

## Falling Wonder

This terrific little toy works because it produces an optical illusion. It makes you believe that you are seeing one thing, although you know you should be seeing something else.

Start with a piece of notebook paper four inches long and about three-fourths inch wide. You'll also need something to draw with—a pencil, a pen, a crayon, or a felt-tipped marker.

About one inch from the left-hand edge of the paper, print a capital letter "S." Draw it almost as high as the paper. If you're using pencil or pen, make the "S" wide and dark. Go over the letter several times, making it wider each time. Illus. 211 shows the "S" already printed.

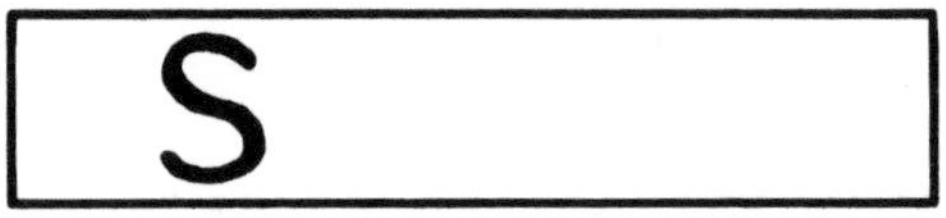

Illus. 211

Illus. 212

Turn the paper over so that the "S" is still at your left. Move to the right and print a capital letter "T." Illus. 212 shows the "T" in place. The dotted "S" shows you the location of the "S" on the other side. Since the "S" is good and dark you should be able to see it through the paper.

Illus. 213

Illus. 214

Again turn the paper over. Now print a capital letter "O" as shown in Illus. 213. The dotted "T" shows you how that letter appears as seen through the paper.

One more time, turn the paper over. This time print a capital letter "P" on the paper an inch or so from the right-hand side. Illus. 214 shows things at this stage.

The dotted lines in Illus. 214 show where to fold up both ends of your *Falling Wonder*. These folds should be one-fourth to three-eighths inch from the ends of the paper. Be sure both folds are exactly the same distance from the ends of the paper, otherwise your *Falling Wonder* won't fall properly. Once the ends are folded up, your finished *Falling Wonder* is shown in Illus. 215.

Illus. 215

Hold the *Falling Wonder* up above your head and then drop it. As it falls toward the floor it will spin rapidly. Look at the spinning toy as it falls. What do you see? Quite plainly you see STOP printed on the paper.

*Falling Wonder* spins so fast that it creates an optical illusion and tricks your eyes into thinking all four letters are printed as one word. Your mind knows that the "S" and the "O" are both on one side of the paper, and that the "T" and the "P" are both on the other. This does not matter. Your eyes tell you otherwise. Try it and see.

Words of four or five letters are just right for *Falling Wonder's* fantastic optical illusion. Why not experiment with a larger strip of paper and slightly longer words?

*Falling Wonder* is great fun and it's sure to make you the center of attention whenever you play with it.

# Looper Ball

This toy will take a bit of time to construct and it will leave your hands good and messy. With this in mind, make sure you cover your working area with plenty of old newspapers so you don't end up with more mess than you can handle.

First blow up a round balloon. You can make the *Looper Ball* any size you wish just by blowing up the balloon to whatever size you wish. Make your first ball somewhere between six and eight inches across.

Blow up the balloon to the proper size and tie the mouth of the balloon so that no air can escape. The best way to do this is just to tie a knot in the balloon's neck. Stretch the neck several times to get it soft and stretchy, then tie it in a knot. If you don't tie knots well, wrap a piece of string tightly around the balloon's neck six times and then tie a firm knot in the string. Whatever you do, don't let air seep out of the balloon. That won't do your *Looper Ball* any good at all.

Now you need to prepare the materials for the papier-mâché you are going to use to cover the balloon. First tear newspapers or paper towels into strips. These strips should be about one inch wide and about twelve inches long.

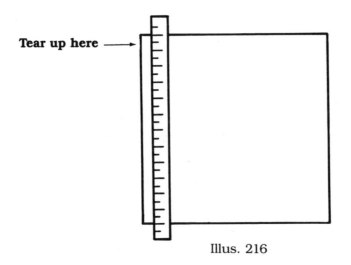

Illus. 216

An easy way to tear paper into strips is to lay a ruler down on the paper as shown in Illus. 216.

Hold the ruler down firmly with one hand. Rip the paper upwards along the ruler's edge. Tear towards the ruler so that the paper is constantly pulled against the edge of the ruler. This will give you a nice, even tear and this method is quite fast. Tear, move the ruler, then tear the next strip.

Tearing works better than cutting when making papier-mâché materials because the rough-torn edges seem to smooth down better than straight-cut edges.

You need paste to turn your torn strips of newspaper (or paper towels) into papier-mâché. Wheat paste, which you can buy in art-supply stores, is great. It comes dry (in a bag) and it turns into paste when you mix it with water. Don't mix an entire bag of paste at once. Mix a little and use it up before making the next batch. Wheat paste tends to get hard if it isn't used quickly.

You can also *make* paste. Start with four tablespoons (two ounces, or 60 grams) of flour. Add six tablespoons

I'm glad you're here. I really didn't want to mess with that hot stove.

(three ounces, or 90 millilitres) of cold water. Mix the water and flour until the mixture is smooth and without any lumps. Now you need to boil one and one-half cups (375 millilitres) of water in a saucepan. BE CAREFUL! This is a good time to have an adult lend a hand.

Stir the flour and water mixture into the hot water in the pan. Turn the heat down low and let the mixture simmer for about five minutes. Then set the mixture aside to cool for at least an hour before using it.

Once the paste is mixed and cool, you're ready to start your *Looper Ball*. Set your balloon on a pad of newspaper so you don't get paste on the desk or table.

Dip a strip of paper into the paste. You want to cover the strip with paste, but you don't want any extra paste on the paper. Slide the strip over the edge of the pan or bowl you're using to hold the paste; rub off any extra back into the container. Illus. 217 show you how to do this.

Illus. 217

Lay the strip on the balloon. Cover another strip with paste and add it to the balloon so it slightly overlaps the first strip. Keep on covering the balloon in this manner. Illus. 218 shows several strips of pasted paper already in place.

Illus. 218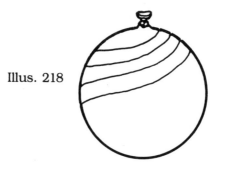

Keep on covering the balloon until the entire thing (except for about one and one-half inches around the balloon's neck) is coated with overlapping strips of paper. Illus. 219 shows the balloon with the first coat of papier-mâché in place. Check the clear space around the neck of the balloon.

Illus. 219

Now begin applying a second layer of pasted paper strips. This time, run the strips in a different direction. This helps stick the strips together and makes your *Looper Ball* much stronger. In Illus. 220 you can see part of the second layer already in place.

Illus. 220

If by now you've run out of time and energy, that's fine. Give the layers of pasted paper a chance to dry and harden. Put your paste in a container that has a tight lid. If you come back to it within a few hours, the paste will still be soft enough to use. Provided the cover is airtight, the paste may still stay fresh for as long as one day.

Keep adding layers of paper until you have a papier-mâché shell about one-fourth to three-eighths inch thick. Use your hands to smooth the paper layers as you apply them. It's messy, so wash your hands often.

Newspaper makes a great *Looper Ball*. However, paper towels are perfect for the last layer. The paper towels smooth down better than newspaper does, since the towels are softer. Also, since the towels are white, you can paint the towel layer. There's nothing wrong, however, with using newspaper for the whole project.

Once you've applied the final layer of paper strips, set the *Looper Ball* somewhere to dry. It may take a day or even two days for the ball to dry completely.

When the ball is dry, puncture the balloon. After the balloon breaks, try to pull it out of the inside of the ball. Don't worry if some sticks to the paper. Just get out as much as possible.

Now you need a handful or even two handfuls of gravel (or something else small and fairly heavy). Fishing-line sinkers and BB's (lead pellets) work fine, but they cost more than gravel.

Squirt a puddle of glue into the bottom of the ball through the opening in the top. Illus. 221 gives you an idea how to do this, in case there's any doubt.

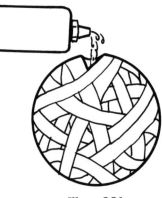

Illus. 221

Keep squirting until you have three or four tablespoons (two ounces, or 60 grams) of glue in the bottom of the balloon. Then drop in the gravel or BB's (or whatever). You can reach through the hole with a ruler or a table knife and move the gravel around so that all of it gets stuck into the glue. If you wish, squirt some more glue on top of the gravel.

The point is to construct a heavy pad made of glue and little rocks; this pad should stick to the bottom of the papier-mâché ball.

Once you have enough gravel in the ball to make the bottom fairly heavy, it's time to seal the top. Use a series of short strips of paper to cover the opening. This part of the ball will be thinner than the rest of the ball, since it will have fewer layers. Illus. 222 shows the patch in place.

Illus. 222

Put on several layers of paper for the patch. Some pieces of paper should be longer than the others so that the top tapers onto the rest of the ball.

Prop the ball against something (so that it stands upright) until the glue inside dries. Meanwhile, the patch will dry and your *Looper Ball* is ready for a trial roll.

Roll it across the floor and it will behave unlike other balls because of the added weight of the gravel in one side. Toss the ball and be prepared for a strange flight path.

Illus. 223

*Looper Balls* are fantastic playthings for small children. Paint stripes on the ball like those shown in Illus. 223 and the ball traces crazy patterns of color when rolled across the floor.

If you wish, paint on a couple of huge eyes (shown in Illus. 224). Give the ball a nose and a mouth and you'll have a funny face. Children will be delighted because no matter how many times they roll the *Looper Ball*, it will always come to rest with the face upright.

Illus. 224

*Looper Balls* may be made to any size you wish. They are quite hard once they're dry. You can play catch with them or you can roll them safely. Don't be tempted to bat one of these paper balls. It's strong, but not that strong!

## One Puff Does It

Here's another of those terrific toys whose name makes perfect sense once the toy is finished.

Cut a sheet of notebook or typing paper four inches wide and as long as the sheet of paper (about eleven inches).

Fold the paper the long way along the dotted line shown in Illus. 225. Try to make the folded part one inch wide. Don't worry if it is a fraction wider or narrower than one inch. *One Puff Does It* will work just fine as long as the fold is *about* one inch wide.

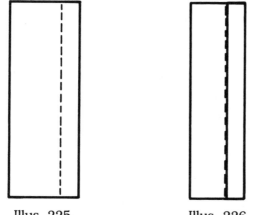

Illus. 225                    Illus. 226

Once the fold is in place, your terrific paper toy looks like the drawing shown in Illus. 226.

Note the dotted line right along the edge of the folded paper. That's your next fold, obviously. Make that fold and you've moved on to Illus. 227.

In Illus. 227 there is another dotted line at the bottom of the paper. Fold up about one-fourth inch of the bottom of the paper so that it looks like Illus. 228.

Now you have just one more fold to go. The dotted line shown in Illus. 228 shows where this last fold goes.

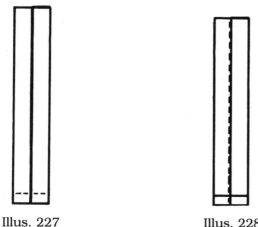

Illus. 227                    Illus. 228

With that final fold in place your *One Puff Does It* is about one inch wide and a bit more than ten inches long. It is shown in Illus. 229. It does not matter after the final fold whether the edge of the final fold of paper is exactly even with the rest of the toy or not. If the edge extends past the rest of the toy, however, then fold it over again.

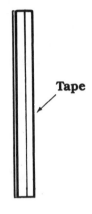

Illus. 229

Run a strip of tape all the way down both sides of the open edge of the paper. The tape is seen in Illus. 229. Masking tape is perfect, but cellophane tape works just fine.

Once the entire edge is taped, your next step is to roll the bottom end of the toy up towards the top. The bottom end is the one you folded up one-fourth inch a few steps back. The top end is still open and stays that way.

Roll the bottom end so that it forms a spiral like the one shown in Illus. 230. Stop rolling when you're about three inches from the top. By now you've probably guessed how this toy works. It's like those popular party favors. Blow into it and it will uncoil in front of you.

Illus. 230

Squeeze the sides of the open end just a bit to form an opening you can blow into. Place the open end in your mouth and give one hard puff. One puff will cause the toy to unwind to its full length. See, it's name does make sense, doesn't it?

So long as you don't get the open end wet and soggy, this toy will last for more than one blowing. Just coil the end into a spiral and blow. It will extend time after time.

If you want, use a longer piece of paper to make a puffing toy longer than the one you just constructed. You can glue or tape two pieces of notebook paper together if you decide to go for a longer length. Lightweight, tough, and thin paper (such as that used for gift-wrapping) makes a toy you can inflate easily.

# Index